From EAST *to* WEST

TEXTILES from G. P. & J. BAKER

GP
&
JB

From EAST to WEST

TEXTILES from G. P. & J. BAKER

Victoria & Albert Museum 9 May-14 October 1984

Exhibition organised by G.P. & J. Baker Ltd
and the Department of Textiles and Dress
of the Victoria and Albert Museum

Exhibition designed by Ivor Heal

Catalogue designed by Bridget Heal

Phototypeset and printed by
Balding + Mansell Limited, Wisbech, Cambs

Published by G.P. & J. Baker Ltd

ISBN 0-9509296-0-3

COVER 248d NYMPHEUS, *screen-printed linen, from Bakers' current range based upon cat. 19, a Chinese Ming Dynasty screen painted on silk, dating from the 15th-16th century* AD.

Contents

"G.P. Baker of the Irises".
A photograph from Picture Post *May, 1949.*

Foreword

When it was first suggested, by whom I'm not too certain, that we should have an exhibition of Baker Textiles over the last 100 years or so, I really had not much idea as to what it was all going to entail.

Over the past two years I have realised there was far more in it than met the eye and I am quite certain all those who have been involved in putting the exhibition together must have come to the same conclusion! As time has gone past, one has thought of more incidents, anecdotes and items that must be included and had they been left out the story would have been incomplete. I hope sincerely that most has been put in but even at this moment further photos or possessions still keep appearing. To have the history and achievements of a company such as ours over a long period of time requires an enormous amount of research and patience and I, for one, am amazed at the lengths and detail everyone who has been involved, has gone to.

I am also quite fascinated at the things that have come to light and even facts about my own family, of which I was not completely aware, and I hope that I have been helpful in confirming some of the anomolies that have cropped up from time to time. I know for a fact that we imported Attar of Roses into this country at one time, when I do not know, but I once had a small bottle in the bottom drawer of my desk, together with various samples of printed velveteen – very useful for polishing my shoes, but which proved to be our only examples of block printed velveteen of that period!

I well remember a rather amusing incident which occurred about 1950 when my grandfather G.P. Baker was rewriting his book, *Mountaineering Memories of the Past*, and I was helping him. It was about that time that a University team from I think Oxford had climbed Mount Ararat and had reported that they thought they had found signs of the ark near the summit. G.P.B. had read this report in the paper and made the remark "Absolute nonsense, there was no trace of it in 1878!" Bakers telegraphic address has been ARARAT LONDON to this day, and I think this incident shows how clear his mind was up to the day he died.

Anyway my very grateful thanks to the Director of the Victoria & Albert, Sir Roy Strong, for letting us put on such an extensive exhibition for so long and to the Keeper of the Department of Textiles and Dress, Miss Santina Levey, for sparing four members of her Department to work so intensively for over two years; we are very honoured and privileged.

Then to Natalie Rothstein for her great idea of starting with the carpet connection – I know G.P. Baker gave her the idea, but she researched it so thoroughly! To Wendy Hefford, Linda Parry and Frances Hinchcliffe for the parts they have played on each of the periods they have been responsible for and for Linda again on all the research into the Baker Family History (we did have moments when we could not sort which of the great aunts and uncles were which!).

Then to Ann Lynch in the Baker Studio and in fact to all the girls in the Studio who have been so patient whilst the place was turned upside down, looking for a document or a record sample and, of course, to Audrey Duck, who has untiringly washed and repaired old documents and dirty old record samples so carefully and with such skill. My thanks also to my cousin, Martin Baker, who produced so many items connected with our grandfather's life and his father's before him.

Lastly to Ivor and Bridget Heal, who have mounted the exhibition and produced the catalogue respectively with such flair and taste.

I hope you all will enjoy the exhibition as much as I have enjoyed being involved with it and that it will remain in your memories for years to come.

MICHAEL CUTCLIFFE

Loading a camel (see p.14) The bale wrapping (12) would have been used in this way. Photograph by A. Cecil Edwards, reproduced by courtesy of his son, Mr Arthur Edwards.

G.P. & J. Baker – a prologue

Trade with Turkey

THE 1907 PROSPECTUS OF THE NEWLY formed public company of G.P. & J. Baker Ltd, described "the carpet business built up by the personal labours of the partners of the firm . . . forming a connection of Weavers and Agents for the Manufacture of carpets in every important centre of Turkey in Asia, India and Persia".[1] At the first ordinary meeting of August 2nd 1907 the secretary, R.F. Davis, explained "the carpet branch of the business was originally established about 30 years ago . . ." and he described it before dealing with "art furnishing fabrics". In actual fact trade with Turkey began when George Baker senior received his first parcel of English linens to sell for his brother in the middle of the 19th century.

Turkey in the late 19th century

George Baker arrived in Turkey in 1847 at a critical point in Anglo-Turkish relations when Sir Stratford Canning, cousin of the former prime minister George Canning, had returned to Constantinople as British ambassador. With considerable success Stratford Canning sought to ensure that British influence in Turkey became and stayed paramount over that of France, Russia or any other country. The major preoccupations of the years 1845–47 were the settling of the frontier with Persia[2] and Stratford Canning wrote of the difficulties "attached to every question of a religious character between the two adverse sects of Mohametanism"[3] and, secondly, "restoring tranquility and satisfying if possible the interested parties in Mount Lebanon."[4] It "might be better for the present state of affairs that the American squadron should not appear on the coast of Syria".[5] These affairs of state were carried on by an embassy and staff scattered across Constantinople for the embassy had been burnt down in 1831 and rebuilding only properly started again in 1843. A second fire in January 1847 destroyed the embassy chapel – and some of the building materials for the main embassy – causing yet more delays. Both the politics and the fires were relevant to the fortunes of the Bakers.

Turkey was a backward country with a shaky economy, a doubtful currency, and a weak army. Part of the rebuilding problems arose because the Turks were unused to written contracts. It was a country which tolerated slavery until the 20th century and which at times savagely persecuted its minorities – though Charles Edwards wrote to G.P. Baker on May 9th 1876 that "the poor Turk dreads Christians murdering them as much as the Christians fear".[6] Nevertheless, the potential of the Turkish empire as a market was foreseen in an Embassy dispatch referring to "The prospects which are opening to our trade in the Eastern part of this empire and the importance which may justly be attached to the free navigation of its great rivers . . .".[7] Attempts were made in 1846 to bring railways and steam while Stratford Canning was interested in the establishment of a commercial bank at Smyrna[8] and in getting postal agreements. "The right of British subjects to participate in the retail trade" of the country was important (but the embassy fully agreed that traders must not sell the local population alcoholic spirits!). Even its political problems could be of benefit to the trader. The crisis on the eve of the Bulgarian revolt in 1876 nearly brought to the Bakers an order for 40,000 waterproof inverness capes with hoods for the Turkish army – but the Turkish authorities could not raise the deposit of a quarter of the price in gold.[9] The change of Sultan led Charles Edwards to write hopefully to G.P. Baker of the prospects of selling brass bedsteads to the new harem.[10] The British community in Constantinople was influential but not large in the middle of the 19th century for the question was discussed in the light of the size of the rebuilt chapel to hold 300 people. Apart from embassy and consular staff dealing with important questions throughout the empire there were Scottish engineers in the service of the Porte (said to be Presbyterians who would not use the chapel) and a growing merchant community of whom George Baker soon formed a part.

Outside Turkey European views of the Turk varied between an image of total oppression and the wildly romantic (cat. 11). As traders the Bakers preferred to see the empire prosper. The Turkish viewpoint was similarly ambivalent. Although a few foreign educational establishments like Robert College were tolerated, contact with foreigners was regarded with suspicion. Communities lived largely within their own districts and yet European influences were seeping in. There were English and other European governesses and teachers, while men in Constantinople were increasingly wearing European dress. Children also often wore this, for the Bakers were exporting little girls' dresses and boys' sailor suits. There are references to the music of European composers, to the influence of the French theatre and, from the correspondence of G.P. and still more James Baker, we have a picture of some really useful European exports, metal bedsteads, mosquito nets, medicine, umbrellas, grain sacks, and tents among them.

Constantinople was (and still is) a beautiful city in a fine situation with panoramic views, a city of ancient monuments from the Theodosian walls to the 16th-century Mosques – its beauties are, however, never mentioned in the Baker letters. The weather is another matter, for the centre of

Constantinople became unbearably hot and steamy in summer and it was both cold and wet in winter. The memoires of the European community present a picture of an idyllic life set against a background of political violence and unrest.[11] Cheap living, summer residences on the Bosporos or the islands of Marmora, good food, picnics, cycling(!) football (F. Baker played on December 23rd 1890 for the Asian Side residents) regattas (G.P., Henry, and James all rowed in them), promenading, balls for visiting naval squadrons and even an occasional royal visit enlivened society. There was a darker side. When George arrived the embassy were sending home periodic reports on the advance of cholera. After one of the frequent and disastrous fires in the city the *Levant Herald* reported[12] "a number of English ladies have formed themselves into a working branch of the British sub-committee, and are collecting, making and distributing clothing with excellent effect. The depots . . . are at Mrs Baker's, 7 & 9 Kule Kapisi and at Mrs Knight's . . .". On February 25th 1876 Charles Edwards wrote to G.P. "Mother keeps well and is doing Hercules work for the Dorcas this year . . .".

By 1849–50 work on restoring the embassy had reached a sufficiently advanced stage for the Treasury to be accusing the Surveyor, W.I. Smith, of "reckless extravagence" in dealing with the interior fittings.[13] Stratford Canning wanted English furniture but neither he nor his predecessor Lord Cowley wanted either a glazed roof to the centre courtyard or a terrace with balustrade – both of which were built and survive to this day with a garden whose design may reflect George Baker's work. The cost of building stone was very high. However, Canning did think he could dispense with a throne! Some of the craftsmen and technicians who came out to do this work became closely involved with the Baker family (see below). Partly at G.P.'s suggestion, made in August 1886, his youngest brother, James, joined him in the Autumn of 1887 to work "in the importation business" while their brother Arthur had already started helping his father. After initial doubts about him "this business is too much for Jim and we must make other arrangements"[14] G.P. accepted his brother and was able to write to his father "my sole attention now is carpets and general supervision."[15]

Exports to Turkey

Initially, George Baker was largely concerned with the export of textiles from England as well as other useful goods. When Baker and Hayden opened a second shop in 1867 (207 Grand rue de Pera) in addition to their shop at 2 Kule Kapisi they advertised textiles, ironmongery, boots, shoes, luggage, baths and showers and sewing machines.[16] After the dissolution of the partnership "Baker's improved sewing machine" was an eye-catching feature of his advertisement, changed later for "Baker's perfection", a lock-stitch machine. Other machines sent out included wringing and mangling machines and a knife grinding machine (with legs-broken on the voyage). George senior was less concerned to send Turkish goods to England. No

LEFT *Advertisement in the Levant Herald, Saturday August 31st, 1872*
CENTRE *Dividable piano, sketch from letterbook March, 1888 p.799.*
RIGHT *Scent fountain, sketch from letterbook April, 1888 p.832.*

letters have survived from the 1850s but in the 1870s it seems as if he normally paid for his goods with bills of exchange although an occasional parcel of Turkish embroidery was also sent. Almost all the goods sent out in 1886–8 for which a complete letter book has survived were still textiles but the range had widened: worsted vestings, army cloth, bell tents, padded drills, shirts, oil-cloth, "hygiene blankets" (washable), mackintoshes and other waterproof clothing and galoshes, "curtain vitrages", Nottingham lace curtains (already featured in the 1870s), plushes, piano covers etc. etc., all things essential to a Victorian household in England but evidently also in demand in Turkey. More esoteric but equally redolent of the times were a piano divided into four pieces for shipping which James sketched and a rather clever idea, a scent fountain which James thought would be a suitable present "for the palace". When they could, they preferred to meet the orders from Turkey from goods on the market but it was seldom possible and they had frequently to have goods specially made[17] (see below).

Exports from Turkey

By the mid 1870s some Turkish goods were being sent to London. There were sets of curtains and furniture sets on order "in shape of those you sent me" as well as "tea cozzies".[18] The firm opened yet another new shop, 500 Grand rue Pera, for which gas fittings were being sent out from England. On March 17th 1876 Charles Edwards wrote to G.P. ". . . the carpet trade I am bearing in mind and trying to find a man that can serve as a source of the intermediate export for I fancy the goods will always come nearly 10% above the Smyrna prices . . . but this is one branch of what I sincerely hope may become an export trade". It would also be necessary to get a good house in England and buy for them or "sell on sample". G.P. did not immediately react apparently and it seems likely that it was his journey to Persia (see below) in 1878 which finally decided them to engage in this trade, cat. 13 is a tangible memento of the trip. G.P.'s respect for Oriental Art was to culminate in his great book *Calico Painting and Printing in the East Indies in the XVII–XVIII centuries* published in 1921 – which cat. 16 is illustrated on pl. 20. By 1886–8 the import of carpets had become the lifeblood of the firm until, in 1892, George senior separated the carpet account from other business giving both James and G.P. £5,500 to carry on this trade. The import of carpets continued to be of the greatest importance although since overshadowed by their work in the printing of textiles in England for a European market. They imported Persian, Turkish, Caucasian and Turkoman carpets, some for re-export to Paris and the United States. The survival of so much correspondence sheds important light both upon the carpet trade and upon the carpets themselves. Their second line were embroideries though these were far less important. We learn about their customers,[19] their competitors[20] and their agents.[21] We learn not only from whence the carpets came but which were the most popular in England and their price. We see the problems of the trade and learn, above all, how far they were able to get carpets made in several different places to their colours and to their patterns.

Oriental carpets

From Persia they imported Carabaghs, Khorassans, "Kains", Herats including "antique Herats", Kirmans including some "Indian design"[22] some in Herati design and some "Shah Abbas in fine quality",[23] Mesheds and Kurdish rugs. Tabriz and Hamadan are seldom mentioned although it was in Hamadan that the firm subsequently established a factory. The bale wrapping Cat. 12, may be a by-product of this trade. The most frequently mentioned Caucasian rugs are Kazaks, Daghestans and Sumacs, "Bokharas" are not differentiated by tribe but they imported saddle-bags as well as full-sized carpets. From Turkey itself they took Ushaks, Kilims, some from Aleppo, Ladiks and "antique Ladiks", "Anatolians" occasionally Ghiordes, Koulas and some not very easy to interpret such as Shivas, Sapkelis[24] and "Zapraks Circassian design".[25] They frequently imported "Turkey Stair"[26] and were cross when the measurements varied. Such carpets can be seen in fashionable paintings – although it is impossible to say whether the artist depicted the machine-made European versions of oriental designs or the original and the two could be very close. Occasionally, G.P. sketched what he wanted. Some Oushaks, 11 × 5 ft, had two bands at each end ". . . say all the plain of old gold or terra and the bands across of darker colour mixed effects and of the work made at Oushak".[27] The sketch does not suggest in any way the modern carpet connoisseur's idea of an Ushak carpet of any date. Another hopeful line were "billiard surrounds".[28]

Some types of carpet known today such as Mudjur or Melas among the Turkish carpets hardly appear while Shirvan carpets were not in demand according to a letter of September 22nd 1886. Others like the Zapraks seem to have been among their most popular lines. An occasional influence from their oriental interests can be seen in the later production of printed textiles as in cat. 175. It is possible that the Bakers imported the "missing" types under more generic names.

Although the carpets were hand-made in remote villages or by nomadic tribesmen and then carried in bales by camel, the Bakers expected the results to conform precisely to their orders. Exact sizes were given and orders rejected if they were more than an inch or so out. There are frequent references to required colours and to "new designs". In May 1886 G.P. wrote to his father about an "exclusive design of seven colours" from Ushak.[29] He wanted samples in two qualities and then would "treat for a quantity of 100/150 carpets". He contemplated similar "business in Koulas and Guerdes". In December 1886 G.P. explained to his father "if we can't get the Daguestan people to make new goods to my colourings we shall give up these goods".[30] Kirmans on order must have colourings "like the original samples . . . with the exception of the borders which may vary. The originals I keep to take orders upon".[31] Designs were referred to by number "1 Oushak 6810, border plain, blue centre colour of sample enclosed . . .".[32] The source of such patterns could be oriental carpets which were selling well. G.P. was, however, very conscious of machine production in England. Thus he wanted "subdued tones after the style of some Templeton rugs you will see in our store in Constantinople, imitation of Ghiordes, color is of greater importance than design".[33] In some Kirman carpets of different sizes "vary the borders in above and in cream ground try some of the effect as in the table-cover sent. My present cream ground sample is weak in the figure . . . the outline, light blue, making it washy – I sent a tracing today . . . in Templeton's original it is as I require".[34] Perhaps in some ways it seems even more remarkable that among the goods shipped to Turkey were Crossley's carpeting[35] as well as Brussels and "royal Axminster with Border".

There were recurring problems: goods arrived late or not at all, sizes and colours were wrong, carpets arrived moth-eaten or too coarse, or they were good but expensive. He was continually worried about competition. Carpets might be good but wrong for the intended market. He cautioned his father "not to be too eager for the Old Persian designs now that they are getting into general hands". The ones he was receiving "are very violent in colours and only useful for the Americans. They rush for them and not the larger designs".[36] He often sold to Bon Marché in Paris but warned La Fontaine "Don't go wharping till you get the Paris confirmation".[37] Moreover, there was a marked seasonal drop in sales immediately after Christmas and in high summer and when this happened there was a cash flow problem. Both G.P. and James frequently wrote to their father for money to settle outstanding bills for goods they were exporting to Turkey. Returns for carpets were always slow.

Embroideries and other goods

Embroideries were very much second in quantity and value but did offer some steady lines. Table-covers, Persian vestings, cushions, d'oyleys, mantle borders, "we should like also a few with the better work, there is an objection to lockstitch work and I think in time we shall only sell the best work",[38] aprons, banner-screens, and collar and cuff sets. Antimaccassars, "antis", appear on most orders though "if you should see Mr La Fontaine I wish you would express our disgust with the Antimaccassars on shantung cloth . . . colouring and work are all bad and quite unsaleable . . .".[39] Just as Templeton machine-made carpets were to guide the designs of hand-made oriental rugs so G.P. sent out in November 1886 "2 patterns of machine embroidery on printed flannel or Cashmere. We want to get the same effect and I think if you go round to your men who sell old cashmere shawls you will find something suitable for designs and ideas". G.P. also proposed to get "some cashmere designs printed in bands on your own cotton cloths".[40] He liked some coloured embroidered d'oyleys sent – very good work – "it will also do for table centres and antis but here the work does not require to be so fine, Machine will do but in good colours".[41]

The range of goods they imported included "real Turkey towels",[42] side-board cloths and napkins "though the crochet work quite spoils the goods",[43] tassels, red and yellow handkerchiefs, scarves, damascene curtains, Scutari velvet (often too expensive), Broussa satin and gold laced portières, and they discussed the import of smoking jackets.

Nevertheless, G.P. was often depressed about the uncertainty of trade. He made a careful balance every six months of the carpets imported from La Fontaine. At times stock accumulated to a worrying level.[44] In April 1888 G.P. thought that the carpet business was in a critical state, "either we do it ourselves or represent SLF and others", and he was casting around for new outlets. He could perhaps get "some of Hampton's business and some of Shoolbred's, all of the stores and with one or two Yankee Commissions there's £500 a year out of it".[45] The trade in Daghestans fell off because the customers preferred to go directly to the docks.[46] After he had taken over general supervision of the business he wrote of his disappointment "with the way in which things are opening up on carpets . . .". He wondered about cotton or silk goods but thought that the latter "had had its day".[47] The next letter book is missing but we know that the outcome of these doubts was the suggestion made by Sydney La Fontaine that G.P. & J. Baker should join an amalgamation of carpet firms. The brothers approved and James became the first managing director of the Oriental Carpet Manufacturers, O.C.M. Starting as James Baker's assistant Cecil Edwards ultimately took over first in Persia and then in London. It is from their factory at Hamadan that the carpet comes which is displayed in the entrance to the exhibition.

A fitting conclusion to the activities of the Bakers in Turkey was the award of the silver medal of the order of Iftihar to George senior in 1902, followed in 1905 by the equivalent order of Sefkat to Maria. Not only was their probity as merchants stressed in the citation but also the Baker contribution to Turkish Society.

NATALIE ROTHSTEIN

The Baker Family

THE HISTORY OF FAMILIES IS complicated and often only of interest to those personally involved. To devote a chapter to this subject is essential, however, for not only could the firm of G.P. & J. Baker not have existed without the Baker brothers but it is due to their ancestors, quite as much as it is through their own efforts, that trading became their way of life. Their business acumen was inherited as well as taught to them and learned by their own experiences.

Letters, documents and three family accounts, written in 1946, 1965 and 1968[1] form the source of historical and anecdotal material for this survey. All of these vary in details and the evidence of letters has been used whenever possible.

George Baker (1822–1905)

George Baker was born in Totteridge, North London in 1822, the fifth of nine children born to Francis and Sarah Baker.[2] Of three sons who survived into adulthood, James, the eldest became apprenticed to Morley and Powell, a firm of wholesale linen merchants and worked his way from errand boy to senior partner. An internationally respected draper, he was asked to join the panel of judges at the 1873 Paris Exhibition. The next son, Francis, became a local tailor in Barnet and George took up his father's profession as gardener. Both James and Francis were better educated than George as his chosen profession involved him leaving school at ten years of age. His first job, as gardener's assistant, was at the home of Judge Butt, and he earned three shillings a week "with perquisites for each wasp's nest destroyed".

George's training as a gardener can be described fully due to the existence of a completed questionnaire from the "Exotic Nursery, Kings Road, Chelsea" filled out in January 1847 by his previous employer Andrew Porter, the chief gardener at Sprotbrough Hall, Doncaster. From Judge Butt's garden George was apprenticed under his father in the gardens of Mr Thoroughgood in Totteridge. As a "journeyman" he spent a year with Mr Virgo, a nurseryman at Wonersh, Guildford (Virgo was the family name of Sarah Baker, his mother) and one year at Horsham in Sussex. He spent six

George and Maria Baker photographed in Turkey at the time of their marriage in 1853.

years as a foreman gardener, first for Lord de Mauley at Canford in Dorset and then at Sprotbrough Hall employed by Sir J.W. Coply. One year was spent in Kentish Town as head gardener before George returned to Sprotbrough "for improvement". The recommendation states that he was well acquainted with "Cropping the kitchen garden . . . management of Walls and other outdoor fruits" but not acquainted with the "formation of Plantations and their Management". He did, however, "have good ideas and some practice in the laying out of Pleasure Grounds, Flower Gardens and Kitchen Gardens" which must have proved useful for his later work in Turkey. Joseph Knight, who owned the Chelsea Nursery, added his own recommendation to that of Andrew Porter's by saying that he believed that George Baker was likely to rise to "the head of his profession, his knowledge being good and his manners modest and good, his industry and trustworthyness cannot be surpassed".

It is difficult to discover how George first heard of the Government job for a gardener in Constantinople. It is clear, from existing correspondence, that Joseph Knight had been asked to recommend someone for the job, although Ruby Gray states that John Wallace, the husband of George's eldest sister, Elizabeth, was first offered the post, but declined this in favour of one in California. However, George secured the post and set out in 1847 to assist in the laying out of gardens at the British Embassy's Summer residence at Therapia, on a piece of land on the Bosporus "of great beauty" recently given to the British by the Turkish Government. From England George took with him plants to be used in this garden and a collection of fruit trees for the Sultan, Abdul Medjid, which he delivered personally. At the time George kept a notebook, listing in it soil recipes and other items referring to his work. By April 1849 his list of fruit trees "grafted at Therapia" is substantial including apricots, peaches and pears and he is said to have introduced the wisteria to Turkey by first planting it at Therapia. Within a few years George Baker was also employed to help replan the garden of the new British Embassy in Constantinople being rebuilt to replace that previously burned down. Various tradesmen were brought out from England at this time to assist in the building and decoration of the new embassy and George became friendly with a number of these men, including Henry Pulman (an architect, who under Sir Charles Barrie, had been employed by the Office of Works to look into the costing of the enterprise) and four traders called Hayden, Haywood, Burness and Duff who were all to remain in Constantinople on the termination of the embassy work in order to set up their own businesses. George had also begun to look outside the embassy for interest and profit and quite soon after arriving in Turkey he had started a small private nursery dealing in plant cuttings. An opportunity to quit gardening came when he was asked to go as foreman on the Mesapotamian Archaeological Expedition under Austen Layard and Richard Burton, but the expedition was delayed and George decided to stay

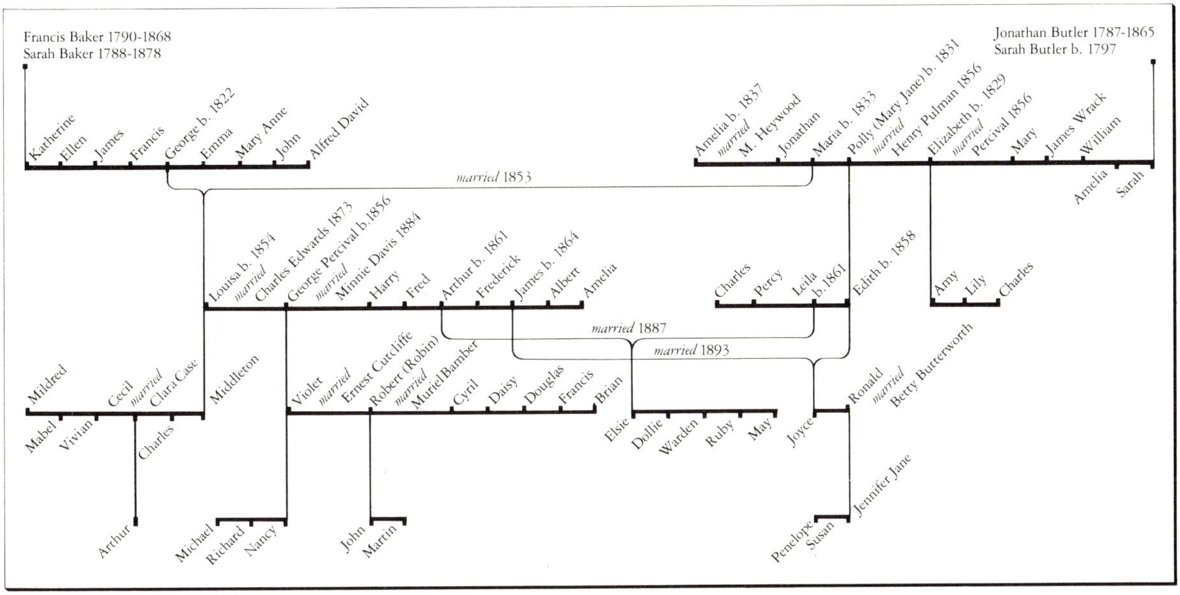

Family Tree of the George Baker family (only members specifically mentioned in this chapter, or who worked for the Firm have been included).

in Constantinople. The possibility of setting up as a trader had already attracted him and he had met his future wife, Maria Butler.

Maria Butler (1833–1908)

Jonathan Butler, a ship's carpenter from Hull, and his wife Sarah had ten children of which at least five are known to have survived beyond adolescence; one son James (born in 1825) and four daughters, Elizabeth (1829), Mary Jane (Polly) (1831); Maria (1833) and Amelia (1837). In 1850 or 1851, on the recommendation of William Rennison, James's brother-in-law, Maria set out for Constantinople to become governess to the children of Alexander and Eliza Baltazzi, a wealthy Greek banking family. It is likely that George and Maria met soon after Maria had reached Constantinople and she became the first of three Butler sisters to marry and settle in the city. Maria was twenty when she married George Baker and a letter of consent was sent by her father. Having not met his future son-in-law, nor knowing the conditions or manner in which his daughter was to live, this letter, dated February 3rd 1853, is a touching, gracious one, which finishes "I hope and trust that you will both be happy and never have to regret that you have made the choice of my daughter Maria is the wish and will be the prayer of your friend and well wisher Jonathan Butler". The couple were married at the Chapel of the British Embassy on May 26th 1853. The register was signed by George Butler, Eliza Baltazzi, William Rennison and Amelia Butler.

Maria's sisters, Polly and Amelia, followed her to Constantinople, Polly replacing Maria as governess to the Baltazzi family. In 1856 she married Henry Pulman, and a little later Amelia married M. Heywood, whom they had met at the home of George and Maria Baker. Elizabeth, Maria's eldest sister, remained in England and in 1856 married, in Bradford, the husband of one of her deceased sisters, a man called Percival. The Heywood, Percival and Pulman families were to play an important part in the lives and business interests of the Baker family.

George Baker as Trader

By the mid 1850s the development of trading in imported British goods, both within the European community and with the Turkish population of Constantinople, had accelerated. George Baker, with a number of important contacts in the city realised the potential of such business and sent for a small shipment of linens from his brother James. These were quickly sold to the British Embassy and the order was repeated. In 1857 a room was taken in Pera to house the stocks of imported goods. In 1860 George went into partnership with Hayden, whom he had met when they both worked at the British Embassy, and goods were supplied on demand; James Baker acting as agent and shipper in London. By August 1862 George had given up his job as gardener and a shop was opened below the Galata Tower. George Baker was, clearly, a hard-headed and successful businessman although no balance sheets were kept of this early trade. Credit was offered, and all prices included a mark-up of 75 per cent on the cost of the purchase of goods in England (packing and shipping were included). The diversity of goods imported and sold has already been described and although choice was limited usually to two brands or types of each object, trade went from strength to strength. George began to invest in other local businesses, including the flour mill managed by his brother-in-law, Heywood, and by 1869 the Baker-Hayden partnership was dissolved in favour of separate businesses. In 1870 George Baker opened another shop in Pera and this provided the nucleus of the general trading companies variously known as Baker and Edwards, Edwards and Sons and G. & A. Baker Ltd, which continues to trade in Turkey today.

The George Baker Family

George and Maria Baker had nine children, of which two, Frederick born in 1859 and Albert, born in 1868, died in infancy. All the children were born in Turkey and their various registrations[3] give some indication of the family's whereabouts and their father's trading status at each birth. The first five children, Louise (born in 1854); George Percival (1856); Henry (Harry) (1857); Frederick (1859) and Arthur (1861), were all registered on August 16th 1862 by George Baker "merchant of Galata". Louise and George Percival were born in Therapia and the others in Pera. Frederick William (1862) was born at Galata and James (1864) and Amelia (1866) at Pera, their father describing himself as both "general dealer" and "general merchant".

George Percival Baker's memoirs of childhood are anecdotal but give a fascinating insight into the life of Europeans living abroad. "Their existence" described by Ruby Gray as "having a strong English middle-class Victorian flavour with unexpected Eastern sidelights". Summers were spent by the Baker family on the island of Halki in the Marmora Sea and G.P. Baker remembered his parents' first home, at the Galata Tower near to the homes of the Heywood and Pulman families.

Education

As the eldest son, G.P. Baker's education was experimental. From attending a Franciscan monastery where he could remember learning some Italian, he went, at the age of eight, to a school at Taksim, near the British Embassy. Run by a schoolmaster brought especially by the British community to Turkey in 1863, lessons were held in a large marquee left over from the Crimea War.

In 1866 Louise and G.P. were brought to England and Louise, who was twelve, was enrolled at a boarding school in Sydenham, her brother going to school close by, in Upper Norwood. Within a year Harry had joined his brother in England and another school was found for the boys. In the holidays the boys lived with their aunt Polly Pulman, who was now widowed and living in Balham with her children Edith, Leila, Percy and Charles, close to her widowed sister Elizabeth Percival and children Amy, Lily and Charles. The Pulman house became home for G.P. Baker throughout his school days and early years in business. He was very fond of

The five sons of George and Maria Baker, photographed about 1900. From left to right standing; Henry (Harry), James (Jim), seated; Arthur, George Percival (G.P.), Frederick (Fred).

his Aunt Polly who became guardian angel to all the Baker boys as they visited London, and all the Baker, Pulman and Percival children were close friends, with G.P., as the oldest, acting as surrogate father to his cousins. This responsibility must have aged him beyond his years and, as Ruby Gray remarks, "he kept this feeling of family responsibility all his life, he was always ready to help anyone in the family, although perhaps apt to be overbearing at times, but his integrity was never questioned".

Harry Baker made good progress at school and, at the age of eighteen returned to Constantinople to work with "Uncle Heywood" in the mill. Eventually he took sole charge and remained there until his untimely death from cholera in 1906.

The opening of an American school (later to be called Robert College) at Roumeli Hissar on the Bosporus enabled the younger Baker sons to be educated in Turkey, although all finished their studies in England. Arthur studied French and commercial subjects at London University and in France, in preparation for entering the business in Constantinople, where he returned in the early 1880s. In 1890 his father took him into partnership, and the firm of "G. & A. Baker" was started.

Fred, who came to England with Arthur in 1876, stayed for the rest of his life becoming a successful businessman in the City of London after finishing school.

James (Jim) the youngest son was educated at Robert College, which by this time had become the most influential school in Turkey. After a short training with his father in Constantinople he journeyed to London in 1887 to help his brother George Percival, in the London office of the Baker company.

In Constantinople another name had entered the business, that of Charles Edwards, a naval architect, the husband of Louise Baker. Although instructor at the Naval College in Halki at the time of their marriage in 1873, he soon joined his father-in-law's business. He was subsequently taken into partnership which lasted until 1890 when George Baker and Charles Edwards set up separate firms, "G. & A. Baker" and "Edwards & Sons". The Edwards family, Charles and his sons Middleton and Cecil, were to be prominent traders in their own right specialising in the export of oriental carpets with interests in the later O.C.M. company already described.[4]

The London Company

In 1874 James Baker died and G.P. Baker, his nephew, was sent to London to take his place as agent to the Constantinople firm. Although only eighteen at the time he had already spent three years working with his father in Turkey. "For the next four years" he wrote "I remained the agent to the firm, engaged in executing indents and seeing to the shipments, besides receiving consignments of various produce".

For his twenty-first birthday in 1878, G.P. was given three months leave from the firm and money to travel. This holiday, which was spent in Persia, is significant not only for the climbing of Mount Ararat but also as the start of his lifelong hobby of collecting alpine plants. Travelling for part of the time with his father, George, the two men realised the potential market involved in importing Eastern carpets into England and visited manufacturers and agents willing to supply to them. The development of this side of the business was to prove vital financially, both to the welfare of George Baker's business in Constantinople and to the eventual establishment of the firm of G.P. & J. Baker in London.

The increase of the family's business in the 1870s must be due in no small way to G.P. Baker's hard work in London. In 1876 premises were taken at 35 Milk Street, and *Kelly's Directory* lists the occupier as "George Baker – Commission Agent" and a year later as "Levant Shipper". From 1879, on G.P.'s return from Persia, he began to trade in his own name and his father's was dropped from the trade directories. G.P. Baker, who described himself as "Levant shipper . . . carpet manufacturer and wholesale dealer" and "carpet importer" does, however, suggest that he was also agent for the Constantinople business by occasionally listing this in brackets. This description continues in trade directories until a further expansion of the business in 1886 necessitated a move into larger premises, a warehouse at 19 Ivy Lane, off Paternoster Row. The organisation of these premises, with carpets on the ground floor (under the management of James, and later Percy Pulman) and textiles and other "soft goods" above (run by G.P. Baker and later Charlie Percival) flourished until 1893 when G.P. took his brother into partnership.

James Baker (1864–1944)

A great deal of information about Jim Baker can be gleaned from family letters and his enthusiastic, sunny disposition is very evident. At times this was misconstrued by G.P. Baker as Jim's lack of responsibility and it is significant that he did not feel Jim mature enough to offer him a partnership until he (Jim) was twenty-nine years old.

On arriving in England in 1887, Jim joined the London Rowing Club and was one of the winning crew of the Grand Challenge Cup at Henley that year. Rowing was an important part of his life and he spent one and a quarter hours rowing each evening after leaving the office at 5.30 pm. In later life his great hobby was golf.

Despite G.P.'s suspicions, Jim's business sense developed, and by 1907, when the carpet company O.C.M. was formed, it was decided that he should run the firm and look after Baker's interests invested in the new company. A few of his letters from this period survive and show his ability as diplomat and astute businessman to deal with difficult trading obstacles.

In 1894 Jim married his cousin Edith Pulman (Arthur having previously married her sister Leila in 1887) and the couple had two children, Joyce and

Mr and Mrs G.P. Baker's garden at "Hillside", Sevenoaks in Kent. Laid out by G.P. Baker in 1926 this became a centre of interest for horticulturalists. TOP LEFT *Building the rockery, where many prize alpine plants were grown.* RIGHT *Mrs Baker collecting blooms for the house.* BELOW *A rock pool with irises.*

Ronald. Ronald himself joined G.P. & J. Baker and for many years ran the London office. He was also responsible for buying historical textiles for the firm's archives after the retirement of G.P. Baker and was responsible for the development of the company's design studio. He had two daughters, Jane and Penny – Jane spent some time working for the Firm.

George Percival Baker (1856–1951)

In 1884 G.P. Baker married Minnie Davis and they had seven children. Daisy, the second daughter, died in infancy, and three sons died tragically from the effects of war; Douglas and Cyril[5] being killed on active service in 1916, and 1917 and Francis (Frank) dying some years later. The two remaining sons, Robin and Brian, were both employed by G.P. & J. Baker at Crayford. Robin, after a technical training in Germany went on to run the Print Works, with Brian concentrating on woven goods made there. Robin had two sons, John and Martin. John was sadly killed in a motorcycle accident during the Second World War and Martin followed his father as Manager of the Works, having first worked his way up learning all aspects of manufacture.

Violet, the eldest child had three children; Nancy, Dick and Michael Cutcliffe. Michael, like his cousin Martin, joined Baker's after the war and they learned the business together at the Print Works. Michael Cutcliffe is Export Sales Director of G.P. & J. Baker for English speaking countries. He is the only member of the family to have remained with the Firm since it was acquired by Parker Knoll in 1964 and he has special responsibilities for the Design Studio and acquiring textile documents for the archives. Dick joined the Firm for a few years and worked both in London and at Crayford.

Mountaineering and Gardening Interests

Despite G.P. Baker's extensive and exhausting business life he still found time for many hobbies which, in his youth concentrated on mountaineering and later on gardening and photography. After climbing Mount Ararat and other notable peaks he was elected a member of the Alpine Club in 1881 and articles in the *Alpine Journal* and his own privately printed book *Mountaining Memories of the Past* (1951) describe expeditions in Austria and Switzerland, the Eastern Caucasus, the Graians, Scotland, Crete, Norway and the Canadian Rockies. His brother Arthur and daughter Violet accompanied him on a number of these expeditions and his sons Cyril and Douglas became keen climbers, Douglas succeeding in scaling Fuji Yama before his untimely death.

G.P. Baker's friendship with George Yeld, a noted horticulturist and mountaineer, introduced him to plant hunting and in 1911, when he gave up climbing, he continued to travel abroad for this purpose. He introduced a number of alpine and other rare and unusual plants into England and won a number of awards from the Royal Horticultural Society including the coveted Reginald Cory Memorial Cup for a hybrid saxifrage. He was a founder member and served as President of both the Alpine Garden Society and the Iris Society. Many of his plants were used in his own gardens, first at "Ivydene" in Bexley and from 1926 at "Hillside" in Sevenoaks, Kent. He is now known chiefly for his hybrid irises[6] and was responsible for replacing a large bed of old irises at Kew Gardens. He gave up hybridising about 1946 and confined his horticultural interests to selling plants for local charities, the church and Boy Scout Movement being particular favourites. He kept working way beyond a natural retiring age and lived to see his ninety-fifth birthday, clearly a remarkable achievement for someone who had lost no opportunity to pack every hour of his life with activity.

LINDA PARRY

1 George Baker: the Early Years
Books, documents, letters and other material relating to George Baker's early years, including his training as a gardener and employment in the British Embassy, Constantinople.

2 George Baker as Trader
Letters, passports, letters of passage and testimonials referring to George Bakers's life and work in Turkey.

3 The Baker Sons
The Baker family tree, letters and other material referring to the upbringing of the Baker family in Turkey, their education and their introduction into their father's business.

4 George Percival and James Baker and the Turkish Trade
Letter book, loose letters and other documents referring to the import and export trade with Turkey. A carpet, made in the Hamadan factory for an offshoot of the parent company is also shown.

5 Swaislands and G.P. & J. Baker
Letters, photographs, sales catalogues and maps referring to the establishment of the firm of G.P. & J. Baker and their take-over of the Swaisland Printing Works.

6 The Baker Family; G.P., James and their descendants
Photographs, press-cuttings, books and other material relating to individual members of the family and their interests, especially G.P.'s achievements as a mountaineer, and his involvement in local affairs.

7 Horticultural Interests
Photographs and other material relating to George and George Percival's interest in gardening.

Pattern-Books and Precursors

Many of the historic textiles owned by G.P. & J. Baker are duplicated in other collections: unique to the Baker Collection are over one hundred volumes of samples and designs, some inscribed and dated, with patterns of the 18th and 19th centuries. When textile printers went out of business, their designs were purchased by others for continued use and future inspiration. So the new firm of G.P. & J. Baker acquired in 1893–4 an inestimable wealth of pattern-books, mainly from the Swaisland Printing Company with a small but significant group from the handkerchief-printers Baker Tuckers, containing not only designs made for those firms, but also patterns which they in turn had purchased from earlier ones, a process which, repeated, handed down designs dating from the 1760s (cat. nos. 26, 33).

Baker Tuckers

The four surviving scrapbooks of Baker Tuckers (cat. nos. 26, 81), arranged haphazardly and containing few inscriptions, are more helpful to the designer than to the historian. In them, however, are important chance survivals, such as fragments of an 18th-century plate-impression not found elsewhere, a design with the name of the Crayford printer John Munns, and original designs for the strange blue-resist prints found in America (cat. 26). Various books of borders in the Baker Collection, particularly useful to handkerchief designers, may have come from Baker Tuckers; but the only other volume marked as theirs is the important "Dudding's Furnitures" (cat. 53), which must have been acquired by John Baker from the upholsterer George Oakley after 1826.

Henry and John Baker, not known to be related to George Baker and his descendants, first occur in London Directories as "silk handkerchief manufacturers" in 1809. After ten years, Henry's name disappeared, leaving John Baker & Co. at various addresses in the City. Between January 7th and 21st 1842 the firm was joined by Joseph, Henry and William Tucker.[1] Some time between October 1846 and January 1847, designs could legally be registered by "Joseph Henry and William Tucker trading under the firm of

Baker Tuckers & Co.". Joseph was omitted in 1857. By 1885 the firm, described as "silk corah and bandana manufacturers, importers of East India and China silk goods", had offices also in Manchester and Lyon. But in 1894 their silk printing works at Tooting had to be sold due to bankruptcy. "Baker Tucker, S. & Co." inhabited their London offices for 1896–7 only.

The sale notice described equipment at Tooting for printing by block, plate and wax processes including forty-five printing tables. Thousands of Baker Tuckers' patterns can be seen in the registered designs at the Public Record Office (Class X). The firm participated in the 1851 Exhibition, with Henry Tucker Chairman of the Jury for specimens of printing and dyeing.

Charles Swaisland (d.1865) and the Swaisland Printing Company

There are three conflicting accounts of how Charles Swaisland set up his Crayford printworks. George C. Haité in 1897 stated:

> "On the River Cray was located Tagg's factory, afterwards known to the whole printing world as Swaisland's. Swaisland was originally himself a designer, of Mitcham. He was famous for printing valencias. Then he took to the shawl-printing and other styles; and in 1844 he had no less than 120 block-printers printing shawls, dress-materials, etc . . ."[2]

Label sewn to a printed shawl, cat. no. 78

The tradition at G.P. & J. Baker's, published by Muriel Clayton and Alma Oakes in 1954,[3] was that Swaisland's works in Crayford were on the site formerly Edward Vint's and earlier occupied by the Wares.[4] Recently, in an article on Swaisland's neighbour David Evans, Stanley Chapman stated that Charles Swaisland was established at Crayford in 1824 on the site where the Davids family's factory had flourished since 1757.[5]

In spite of *Pigot's Directory* for 1826–7, which named three calico printers at Crayford – Tagg and Whitehead, Davids, Taylor & Co., and Charles Swaisland – implying that the Tagg and Davids sites were still occupied when Swaisland was established, Chapman's version must be accepted, being based on a lease in the Kent Record Office.[6] Directories were occasionally belated in recording changes. To account for the other locations allotted to his factory, it is possible that Swaisland, described in 1847 as one of the principal landowners around Crayford,[7] may have purchased some of Tagg's and Vint's land. Certainly he acquired their pattern-books, one of Tagg's and a number of Vint's being still in the Baker Collection.[8] One of these books (V&A loan 3) containing bills and notes of payment by Edward Vint & Co., creates a vivid picture of a manufacturer's requirements in 1809–10. It is here that Charles Swaisland appears for the first time, as a supplier of blocks. Money owed by Vint & Co. to Charles Swaisland for June 25th 1809 to May 25th 1810 was for 11 holly blocks, 142 holly faces, glue for 142 blocks, and one "Pattern & putting on". This item supports Haité's statement that Swaisland began as a designer, though the tiny pattern drawn on the account hardly reveals his talent. Many more facts are needed for the years between this relatively humble work and the establishment of a factory that was to employ 500 hands.[9]

Swaisland seems to have had no direct sales outlet, but engaged his designs to retailers, commission agents, and even to printers such as David Evans (cat. 78). Erratic registering of designs by Charles Swaisland in all three "printed" classes was probably due to the requirements of these clients. An account book for some thirty clients begun in 1830 shows a preponderance of dress prints and shawls over furnishings, silks and woollens over cottons.[10] A dye recipe book of the 1850s confirms a preference for textures which enhanced the "brilliant and judicious selection of colours" praised by the *Journal of Design*[11] in Swaisland's flannels. At the 1851 Exhibition, where he was on the same Jury as Henry Tucker, Swaisland exhibited "printed Chinese velvet furnitures (application plush)", flannels for dresses and barège shawls, winning a Prize Medal for the latter. Many printed shawls of this period were luxury goods, some patterns requiring 550 blocks[12] and the 150 × 6 feet table among the forty-nine printing tables of the Swaisland sale.

By 1864, with no immediate male heir, Charles Swaisland's partner in registering designs was Charles Leonard Stable, also of Crayford. After Charles Swaisland died, early in 1865, the firm became the Swaisland

Printing Company, remaining independent until the sale of 1893 which launched G.P. & J. Baker on their printing career.

The Swaisland designs

G.C. Haité's article quoted above continued: "It was at Swaisland's that most, if not all, of the old-fashioned designers matriculated, in the good old-fashioned manner of apprenticeship". Little, unfortunately, has survived concerning his designers. George Haité, who died when his son G.C. Haité was only sixteen, in about 1872, probably worked for Swaisland as a freelance, along with Charles Hudson (cat. 70). When both these artists were supplying designs, in 1846, a directory named three designers resident at Crayford: William Hubbard, John Henry Taylor and John Philip Wasley. They may, of course, have been working for David Evans. Hubbard's name appears on some of the designs in the Swaisland books of the 1870s.

It seems likely that many of Swaisland's best designs, particularly for shawls, came from France. Some unbound shâwl designs and some in the books have stamps of G. Meynier (cat. nos. 76, 77) and Edouard Hartweck of Paris. The original titles in gold (in most cases obliterated by later black titles) of two volumes of imaginative designs of the 1830s–50s are "French Drawings II" and "III". A manuscript copy of "Rules for the Drawing Shop",[13] donated to the V&A by Ronald Baker, gives instructions "to stick in the proper book all patterns that may arrive from Paris".

These "Rules" show how the books of patterns were to be kept. "The junior of the shop is to make up all books of patterns . . .", to put designs into the F(illing) and H(eading) books; to number and letter for each client patterns going to London and put corresponding patterns in other books; to strike off and colour the grounds of two repeats of patterns "which are to be placed in the Registration folio until a sufficient number are collected – when they are to be written off in the F&H sketch book" and taken to town for registration, a "portion" of each with the registration ticket to be stuck afterwards into a book.

The Baker Collection retains three volumes of these registered strike-offs, 1842–52,[14] and a book with mixed contents (cat. 80) including registrations of 1870–83; twenty-five volumes of designs for shawls and dress fabrics (cat. 76), inscribed with occasional running numbers, dates and names of customers; one hundred unbound shawl designs (cat. nos. 70, 75, 77); six books of designs and strike-offs of handkerchiefs; a broken sequence of numbered printed dress-fabric samples in books dated 1840 to 1854, and several books of miscellaneous samples without identification.

The Swaisland sale catalogue calls these "The Valuable Variety of Patterns for which this firm has held a worldwide reputation for the last century". G.C. Haité, perhaps thinking also of the older pattern-books owned by Swaisland's, wrote "they in themselves constitute a reliable history of Design and printing in England".[15]

The use of the archive by G.P. & J. Baker

George Percival Baker treasured this hoard of pattern-books, summarising their contents in labels (cat. nos. 40, 41, 74, 81); and he also pillaged them, leaving initials and date in place of designs removed for adaptation in the Baker Studio.

On the fourth Baker Tuckers book he noted: "Mostly Turkey Red Handkerchf. style. There are 3 Small Chinese may some day be of use". One of the Swaisland books bears a note: "When dressing gown cashmeres are wanted, here they are". He was particularly appreciative of the sketches in the Haité/Hudson book (cat. 74), stating: "Towards the end there are some 2 colour effects of distorted root stumps in blue greys which appeal to me for present day screen work. At the end, rough treatment of a large pine which some day might be used for all over hangings". These labels seem to be the same date as one that reads "No good for present wants Mar/39".

Use of the archive was steady from the 1890s (cat. nos. 68–71, 75, 79). Stripes and streaked circles of the late 1890s (Block-book B472) derived from chiné patterns of the 1790s in books such as cat. 41 (not the page displayed). Several gaps in the Swaisland books marked G.P.B. have dates in August 1898. One of them may have contained the "Cashmere patt." (Block-book B679) printed in 1899 and again, as a "Bias scarf" in 1936 (Block-book D161). As it was rare for G.P. Baker to describe what he removed, the identification of these designs remains uncertain; but in one case he left the design with his initials beneath it, and the early 1850s dress material with grouped diamond shapes turns up in 1898 (Block-book B573) with similar designs to either side. Several shawl designs were also used, some identified by their original Swaisland number, as with H1143, an unbound design of the 1840s, having "3 grounds cut Dec. 1925".

Mr Martin Baker's notes on a lecture given in 1960 state that the firm continued printing the "Paisley" style "in decreasing quantities until a few months ago". Attempts to revive it in the 1960s were not successful (cat. nos. 73, 75); but recent popularity may see those Swaisland designs once more in production, as Bakers follows the long established tradition of holding fast to good patterns and reproducing them on demand.

WENDY HEFFORD

The Baker Archives

THE ARCHIVES CONSIST OF A wonderful range of textile documents that has been the inspiration for the Baker design studio since the start of the firm. The collection was started by George Percival and James Baker in the early days and additions are still being made when the opportunity arises.

The collection is very varied containing Chinese wallpapers, dresses, church vestments, Peruvian tunics, quilts and curtains. It numbers about 3,000 items, of which 1,883 are of some size, the others being small patterns in the many sample pattern books inherited from Swaislands, who were great collectors of samples books themselves. To all these must be added the Baker record samples, one of each design, numbering over 2,500, plus guard book records of all colourways in the range.

When G.P. & J. Baker joined the Parker Knoll Group in 1964 it was found that the collection of textile documents which had been purchased the year before from W.H. Haynes of Paddington greatly added to the range of the archives, although we now had two pieces of some textiles and there were many that Bakers had printed for W.H. Haynes in the 1920s/30s, Staffordshire Dogs (cat. 67) being one such design.

The oldest pieces in the collection are the Peruvian, one item being B.C. This woven design includes a man holding up two severed heads. The other Peruvian items are mainly 14th century, beautiful geometric designs still in clear bold colours after nearly 500 years. Italian and Turkish velvets, beautiful Indian prints, French toiles, Indonesian batiks, early English glazed chintz prints, plus 18th- and 19th-century dresses, and a 19th-century Persian hat (cat. 13) go to make up this fine collection in which I feel one could say we have something from every century and representing half the world in designs.

The conserving and recording of our archives brings a lot of problems, as the collection is a working one the items are moved around many times. We do have all the larger items photographed now. This saves a lot of time when we wish to find a certain textile. This mammoth task was started before I joined the Company by Flora Ferrara (née Watson), each textile has a photographic number which is also the number now embroidered on to the

34 BIRDS AND FRUIT, *plate-printed cotton, English, Nixon & Co. c.1770*

backing cloth of the item, this number appears again in a record book that tells us where to find that piece. I could not fault this system and was so pleased I did not have to think up a new one, items can be found for a customer to see in a very short space of time.

The Exhibition has helped a lot in tracing designs to the textile document, enabling me to find when one has been used for what cloth and when. My new record filing should now have cross references to find all information.

Although I am not able to do a great deal of conservation I remove the textiles from the brown paper with which they have previously been backed, wash them to remove dirt, dry them on glass and sew them on to a washed cotton backing. As previously mentioned I embroider the reference number on the cotton, so doing away with all pins, staples and ink from the textile item. When finished they are placed in a metal drawer cabinet between acid free tissue paper to await future use in the Studio.

As approximately only half the collection has been used for designs to date, these archives will be a source of inspiration for the Studio well into the 21st century.

AUDREY DUCK
Archivist

Mr Thomas in the Baker Studio at the Swaisland Works c.1910.

Introduction to historic textiles

A SELECTION HAS BEEN MADE OF BAKERS' historical textiles to illustrate both the range of the collection and the use to which it has been put. The contrasting results of different printing techniques has been emphasised by showing several pieces of the same design together. Some textiles are important by any international standard and some simply an amusing reflection of their time. While we cannot write the history of printed textiles in some seventy textiles and ten pattern-books (nor would we wish to do so!) nevertheless, some crucial stages are illustrated from the delicate Indian cotton painting of the mid 17th century and the first clumsy European attempts at block-printing in fast colours. Thereafter we can represent all major developments in technique and some of the high- and low-points in design. In any display of textiles the fragile condition of some precludes the display of a few pieces – but Bakers have looked after their collection so well that this difficulty has seldom arisen.

From 1900 to 1964 the firm of G.P. and J. Baker as well as Arthur, George Percival and Ronald, his nephew, individually, have presented to the Victoria and Albert Museum over 300 designs, block impressions, pattern-books, and textiles, occasionally retaining a less well preserved piece of the same fabric. Many were shown in the 1955 and 1960 exhibitions of English printed textiles to which also generous loans were made. The gifts have also included cat. nos. 9 and 16, reflecting a much wider range of interests. Such generosity to a public institution by a private firm has rarely been matched. The gifts include both historical fabrics and the firm's current productions, now themselves an important part of the history of British textile design. Thus textile designers world-wide who have used the V&A collections in the course of eighty years are in their debt.

We have attempted to show how the firm's Turkish background is enmeshed in their later production in England. Cat. 12 sums this up: a bale wrapping for a bundle of Persian carpets which became the source of a design in 1935.

NATALIE ROTHSTEIN

LEFT 29 CURTAIN, *Plate-printed fustian English, probably J. & M. Ware, Crayford, Kent.*
RIGHT *(top)* 42 *Original design, gouache and watercolour on paper, French, Mulhouse, 1780–90.*
(below) 30 *Resist-printed cotton, English, probably J. & M. Ware, Crayford, Kent.*

8 CUSHION COVER, voided velvet
Turkish; 17th–18th century
44 × 26 (111.7 × 66)

The velvet is woven with crimson cut silk pile on a voided satin ground enriched with silver-gilt thread (bound in 3\1 twill) in the corners of the field, tulips, and the central rosette. The velvet has a point repeat 12 inches wide. There are pious inscriptions in the panels of the border.

There is an inferior copy of this velvet in the Benaki Museum, Athens. These are the only two covers so far known with such inscriptions. The whole group are the subject of a forthcoming publication by Miss J.M. Wearden of the V&A Museum.

Baker No. L079

9 PATTERN BOOK of Silk Ribbons
Greek manufacture in Turkey; first half 19th century
$9\frac{3}{8} \times 6\frac{1}{2}$ (24 × 16.5)

The book is written in Turkish but in Greek characters with details of the number of reels of coloured silk necessary for weaving the samples. These were probably for the home market but are western in inspiration. They may date from the reign of Sultan Mahmud II, son of a Frenchwoman cousin to Josephine Buonaparte. He was a Francophile who attempted to turn Turkish national dress towards European models.

V&A T.671-1919 Given by Mr Arthur Baker

10 Roller-printed cotton
English (?); 1827–30
$39\frac{3}{4} \times 25$ (100.9 × 63.5) REPEAT: $13\frac{1}{16}$ (33.2) × over 25 (63.5)

A galley containing the Turkish admiral rows out to a large sailing ship, the scene contained within a bower of military trophies and flags (those of England, France and Russia) in brown, red, blue and green. The yellow has faded. The scene commemorates the handing over of the Turkish fleet after the Battle of Navarino in which the Turks were defeated on October 20th 1827 – although the detail is inaccurate.
Lit: Hunton, *English Decorative Textiles*, 1930, pl. 89

Baker No. U084

11 ORIENTAL SCENES, cotton litho-printed in purple
French (Alsace, Mulhouse); about 1827–40
Designed by G. Zipelius (1808–90) for Koechlin-Ziegler
$20\frac{5}{8} \times 15$ (52.4 × 38.1) REPEAT: incomplete

A harem scene with a Turk smoking a hookah in the centre. Turkish contact with the west and especially

8

10

12
14

France, was particularly marked in the reign of Sultan Mahmud II. This was reciprocated in a romanticised view of Turkish life, demonstrated in several cottons by this manufacturer.
Lit: Tuchscherer, 1972, pl. 93b. Our design is incomplete and the missing scene appears in this plate.

V&A T.50-1964 Given by Mr Ronald Baker

12 BALE WRAPPING, wool
Persian; second half 19th century
100 × $33\frac{3}{4}$ (254 × 85.7)

Hand-woven in off-white wool, one end is patterned with tapestry-woven bands in brown and black goats' wool, further embroidered in tan and blue with an additional soumak effect in all colours. The other end is stamped "MLN 1174 LONDON MADE IN PERSIA" and there are traces of a stamp possibly applied in Persia. The ends are finished with a warp braid.

Such materials were used for wrapping bales of carpets exported from Persia and can be seen in the photographs taken by Cecil Edwards of camels being loaded in Persia.

Bakers reproduced the patterned end by surface roller in 1935 as "Nomad Stripe" design no. R4625 using a checked pattern to simulate the roughly woven ground.

Baker No. Z044

13 HAT, embroidered woollen shawl fabric;
Persian (Tabriz); 1830s
9 × 7 (22.8 × 17.8)

Dark blue woollen ground with a polychrome floral pattern from a typical shawl edged with a different fabric. It is embroidered in button-hole stitch in white cotton. An original label is inscribed "13,120 GPB purchased in Tabriz 1878". It may have been bought for its pattern but also as a possible sample smoking cap for the British market.

Baker No. K014

14 Block-printed cover
Western India; 15th–16th century
63 × 29 (160 × 73.7)

Cotton printed in red and brown with a simple square within a square, the ground decorated with spots and leaves. The textile came from the burying grounds of Egypt, but its exact provenance is unknown. Indian trade goods were exported all over the ancient and the medieval world and a number have come to light in Egypt.

V&A T.93-1922 Given by Mr G.P. Baker

LEFT 64 *Roller-printed cotton, probably French, c.1835–45.*
CENTRE 46 BORDER, *block-printed cotton, French, Mulhouse, c.1790.*

LEFT 54 *Block-printed cotton, English, c.1815–20.*

RIGHT 52 *Roller-printed cotton, English 1810–20 (see* *also p.59)*.

15 RUMAL (Cover for a ceremonial gift) stencilled, painted and dyed cotton
Indian Golconda; mid 17th century
21 × 25 (53.3 × 63.5)

Light brown ground with scenes of court life possibly alluding to the Persian wine poetry of authors such as Hāfiz, for there are figures reclining on cushions to be served with drinks. The field is filled with flowers, birds and animals. The design is in blue, red, purple, pink, yellow ochre and green. The outer border is white with arabesque decoration between red outer borders.

Bakers printed the design in 1929 by copper-roller, ref no. 2217, width 31 inches, as "Mogul" (R2842). It was screen-printed in 1972 as "Hassan" (A0757).
Lit: Irwin, *Golconda Cotton Paintings*, 1959
Indian Heritage, 1982, nos 239–243

Baker No. G059 (illus. p.44)

16 PETTICOAT, painted, dyed and glazed cotton
Indian Northern Coromandel Coast; mid 18th century
$40\frac{3}{4}$ × 38 (103.5 × 96.5) (fabric) REPEAT: $18\frac{1}{2}$ (47)

The cotton was made for the European market and has large bouquets of flowers with small vases of flowers between luxuriant flowering branches. It has a white ground painted in two reds, two violets, blue, yellow, black and combinations of these colours.

Bakers printed the design in 1925 by copper-roller (X6941) and screen-printed it in 1982 (B0954) as "Curzon".
Exhib: *Metropolitan Museum*, 1927, L2705.26, cat. 347
Lit: Irwin and Brett, *Origins of Chintz*, 1970 cat. 144 pl. 126

V&A I.S.19-1950 Given by Mr G.P. Baker

17 Cotton Batik
S.E. Asian; 19th century
$42\frac{1}{2}$ × 44 (107.3 × 111.7)

Batik in dark blue, brown and yellow. The design is achieved by painting, printing or stencilling the design in hot wax. The textile is then dyed, dried and re-waxed for the next effect. Such materials were primarily intended for clothing.

The zig-zag border inspired a screen-print by Bakers in 1978, "Sumba" (A0893). The internal decoration of the horizontal border and the diamonds is, however, European in character.

Baker No. S003

18 Tapestry-woven woollen cloth
Pre-Conquest Peru: 14th century
$18\frac{3}{4}$ × 25 (47.6 × 63.5) (Max.)

A geometric design of rows of zig-zags in finely woven vicuna on a woollen warp in brown, red, yellow, and white (26 warp threads to inch approximately). There is part of a plain web at the bottom and part of the end border at the top. The precise origin of the piece is unknown.

Bakers screen-printed the design in 1974 as "Bosonova" design no. R1068, see cat. 227.

Baker No. F022 (illus. p.44)

19 SCREEN, ink, colour and mineral pigments on silk
China; Ming Dynasty 15th–16th century AD
$60\frac{3}{8}$ × $30\frac{3}{4}$ (153.2 × 78.2)

Two kingfishers are flying above an egret sheltering below drooping lotus leaves. Large scale bird and flower paintings were used to decorate interiors since at least the Song dynasty (AD 960–1279). Although a recognised theme in Chinese art, bird and flower painting never achieved the same status as landscape art. The most refined style is associated with the Court of the Huizong emperor of the late Northern Song dynasty (AD 960–1127). The refined brushwork and subtle colouring of the early painters set a model for later dynasties – although they were themselves building upon styles already formed in the Tang and early Northern Song dynasties. The mineral pigments, malachite green and azurite blue, were first introduced into China from Central Asia through Buddhist painting. The present work is reduced from a larger format. The composition and brushwork suggest the date.

Bakers have often used this design, see cat. 248 to D.

Lent by the Trustees of the British Museum C. Ptg. 12 OA 1913 4-15.01

20 WALLPAPER
Chinese; First half 19th century
144 × $47\frac{3}{8}$ (366 × 120.3)

Bands of paper $27\frac{1}{2}$ inches wide are joined and painted with gouache. This is part of a set of papers from a house at St Paul's Cray (now demolished). All consist of flowering trees with different birds and flowers and rudimentary rocky landscapes at the base in pale and dark green with pale pink and mauve flowers and a few details in white, yellow, tan etc.

Bakers block-printed a version designed by William Turner in 1922 (P943) and again in 1941, reference R688 and in 1962, reference R885. It was screen-printed in 1977 design no. B0499 in glazed chintz and linen (R1138) and is still in production, always called "Toucans" see cat. 234.

Baker No. V30

22

21 Wallpaper fragment, block-printed paper
English; late 17th century
18 × 16¼ (45.7 × 41.3)

The paper has a staghunt apparently taking place on the outskirts of a village, printed in black, orange and light blue. Several pieces from this paper are known with different provenances. These are in the V & A (E.2232, E.2232a-1974), Manchester, Colonial Williamsburg and elsewhere. This piece came from Aldford House (demolished) Park Lane, London.

Bakers block-printed the design in 1937 as "Park Lane" (A192) and block-printed it again in 1950 (A462) and screen-printed it in the 1970s (B0467). Lit: Oman and Hamilton *Wallpapers* 1982 fig. 30.

Baker No. J073

22 HARPSICHORD, block-printed cotton
Dutch or English; early 18th century
23 × 30 (58.4 × 76.2) REPEAT: 12½ × 10½ (31.7 × 26.7)

The cotton is printed in madder colours, brown and pink, with a tree under which a lady in late 17th century dress sits at a harpsichord, accompanying two recorder players. The primitive state of European block-printing can be seen in the failure to join the repeat properly. The stippled ground is characteristic of the time.
Lit: Jacqué *Mulhouse*, 1978, pl. 57

Baker No. H055

23 Block-printed cotton
probably English about 1750–55
22 × 17 (55.8 × 43.2) REPEAT: incomplete

A "full chintz" with a naturalistically drawn rose branch in two shades of madder red with peonies and other flowers also in two shades of lilac, yellow and combinations of these. A typical mid 18th century furnishing cotton showing the increasing sophistication in technique.

Bakers screen-printed the cotton for export in 1971 as "Rose and Poppy Ogee".

Baker No. H091

24 Part of a chasuble, woven silk
French c.1755–80
17 × 20 (43.2 × 50.8) REPEAT: 10¼ × over 10 (incomplete) (26 × 25.4)

White brocaded silk with a point repeat of a green stem with roses and other flowers in yellow, three shades of blue, three shades of olive green, three shades of pink, yellow and an additional self-coloured pattern in the ground. Tabby with an additional flushing weft. The silk has marks from the former orphreys and is a typical Lyon "ornemen d'église" produced for the church not high fashion.

Bakers block-printed the pattern in 1906 Reference no. B466 as "Gregory's Robe" both as a chintz (F26) and a linen (P82). The self-coloured pattern was changed to blue adding to the gaiety of the design. It is being screen-printed in 1983–4.

Baker No. L017

25 QUILT, resist-printed cotton
English; third quarter 18th century
91¼ (max) × 82¾ (231.8 × 210.2) REPEAT: 26 × 19¾ (66 × 52) half drop

Coarse white cotton, resist-printed and dyed in two shades of indigo blue with a bold pattern of curling branches, leaves and fruit. The quilt is made up from several pieces, stuffed with cotton and lined with white linen. The edges are bound in various tapes typical of those made in and around Manchester for chintz curtains. A plain cotton lining has been added later. Many such resist-printed cottons have been found in the United States – perhaps specially produced for the American market.

Bakers block-printed the design in 1928 as "Holzach Jacobean Blue and White" and screen-printed it in 1971 as "Baroda" (R1022).
Lit: Montgomery *Printed Textiles*, 1970, pp. 194–211, fig. 188a depicts a very similar design in Winterthur.

Baker No. Z067

LEFT 15 RUMAL, *stencilled, painted and dyed cotton, Indian, Golconda mid 17th century.*
BELOW 18 *Tapestry-woven woollen cloth, Pre-Conquest Peru 14th century.*

ABOVE 74 *Sketch for a shawl border, by G. Haité for printing by Swaisland, c.1845–7.*
BELOW 78 *Shawl, block-printed by Swaisland for David Evans, 1859.*

26

26 PATTERN-BOOK once owned by Baker Tuckers (No. 2)
Designs displayed, blue and white resist prints, English, 1760s–70s.
20 × 14 (50.8 × 35.5)

This volume, particularly rich in 18th-century material ("Full of all sorts of good things", as G.P. Baker remarked) contains four designs for a particular kind of blue and white resist print found only in America (see cat. 25). One piece in the Albany Institute of History and Art has an English excise stamp of 1766. This evidence of English manufacture is supported by the presence in this book of English designs of four original designs for this kind of printed cotton. The two displayed show parts of the textiles illustrated in Montgomery figs. 205 and 194; the others correspond to fig. 193 and to the petals only of a flower in fig. 208. A design at the end of the book has the name of John Munns (Crayford, bankrupt 1784) inscribed with a design number: but the scrapbook is too diverse for identification of any other design with Munns.
Lit: Florence H. Pettit, *America's indigo blues*, New York, 1974.
Montgomery, *Printed Textiles*, 1970.

Baker Collection

27 PROVENCE, roller-printed cotton, 1936–7
55 × 32 (39.7 × 81.2) REPEAT: $29\frac{1}{8}$ × 32 (74 × 81.2)

A fragment of a plate-impression on paper of this design is pasted into the Baker Tuckers scrapbook no. 2 (cat. 26). The original monochrome plate-print of Night-flowering Cereus was produced at Bromley Hall in Middlesex from the 1770s to the 1790s. Addition of a ground colour transforms the design. A sample of the Baker adaptation in four colours is in a copper-roller book, No. 2816, with a note that the roller was sent for re-coppering on 1/7/58.

Baker Record Sample No. A161

28 Plate-printed fustian
English; Collins, Woolmers; 1765
19 × 30 (48.3 × 76.2)

Part of a landscape printed in red with the factory's name on the base of a column, and on a fence "H. Roberts sculp." This may refer to the engraver and print seller H. Roberts, born 1710, died before 1790, of Hand Court, Drury Lane, London. Half the design is missing. Nixon's reprinted it in the later 18th century (see cat. 33). The complete design in the Metropolitan Museum shows a ruined arch with a cottage by the side.
Lit: Hunton, *English Decorative Textiles*, 1930, pl. 64; *English Chintz*, 1960, cat. 81

Baker No. U044

29 CURTAIN, plate-printed fustian
English; probably Joseph and Mary Ware, Crayford, Kent; c.1765–70
90 × 77 (228.6 × 195.6) REPEAT: $34\frac{7}{8}$ × $35\frac{1}{2}$ (88.5 × 94)

Delicately drawn birds perch on branches of fruit – plums, cherries and grapes among them – with roses, anemonies, carnations, lilies and convolvulus among the many flowers twined in the branches. The design is printed in black and red with two plates which was both unusual and expensive.

Bakers printed the design in 1939 by copper roller, reference 2932, and again in 1952 as "Fruit and Flowers" (F918 and B186). It was screen-printed in 1970 as "The Ware" (B414).
Exhib: Farnham 1982 cat A.1 pls. 1 and 11

Baker No. Y095 (illus. p.36)

30 Resist-printed cotton
English; probably Joseph and Mary Ware, Crayford, Kent; c.1765–70
$35\frac{1}{2}$ × $44\frac{1}{2}$ (90 × 113) (approximately) REPEAT: $34\frac{1}{4}$ × $33\frac{1}{2}$ (87 × 85)

An unusual reversed and resist-printed version of cat. 29. The design does not fit into the normal blue resist printed textiles described by Florence

Montgomery since the pattern has the appearance of a photographic negative, and the actual technique is still under discussion. The spiders' webs are an additional detail.

Bakers are working on a screen-printed version of the design 1983–84.
Exhib: Farnham, B2
Lit: Montgomery *Printed Textiles*, 1970, pp.194–212

Baker No. A117 (illus. p.37)

31 Plate-printed linen
English; Joseph and Mary Ware Crayford? about 1770
$21\frac{3}{4} \times 31\frac{1}{2}$ (55.2 × 80) REPEAT: $18\frac{1}{4} \times 15\frac{1}{4}$ (46.3 × 38.7)

The linen is printed in madder colours with additional pencilled blue (now faded) with a delicate vertical pattern of flowering alternating with cherry-bearing branches. The use of two copper plates, here red and dark brown was exceptional, hence the suggested attribution. Bakers reproduced the design in 1942 by copper roller and 1978 by screen-printing, see cat. 235.

Baker No.H251

32 SKIRT, plate-printed cotton
English; about 1770. Factory unidentified
H. Hem to waist $36\frac{1}{2}$ plus tape $1\frac{1}{4}$ (92.7 and 2.5)
REPEAT: H. $37\frac{3}{8}$ (94.9)

The skirt is printed on its side in indigo blue with a design epitomising the title of this exhibition. A Turk leads a camel past a hillock taken from contemporary Indian palampores on which grows a coconut palm. Beyond are goats, a horse, a tree on another hillock and some strangely rendered dogs. Along the edge are insects, tortoises etc. There are sundry butterflies, monkeys and birds in the main field. The edge of the plate is visible in the grass beyond the horse.

Baker No. K006

33 PATTERN-BOOK, copper-plate impressions on paper
Nixon & Co., Phippsbridge, Surrey; c.1760–89
19 × 12 (48.2 × 30.4)

Francis Nixon produced the first known plate-printed textiles in Ireland (1752), and in England (by 1756) at Phippsbridge, where his firm remained after his death in 1765, until 1789. Almost one hundred of his designs survive at Mulhouse, of which only eight are duplicated in this book of twenty-two large furnishing designs, only a portion of each being recorded. Subjects are varied, with Aesop's Fables after Francis Barlow, Chinoiseries after Pillement, arborescent designs inspired by Indian palampores, pastoral subjects, naive classical scenes and sophisticated rococo scrollwork. Three designs in the book were taken over from the printworks at Woolmers when Collins ceased business after 1766 (see cat. 28).
Exhib: English Chintz, 1960, cat. 73

Baker Collection

33a BLUE AND WHITE JOUY, copper-roller on cotton, 1951
Based on the Nixon design
50 × 40 (139.7 × 101.6) REPEAT: $37\frac{3}{4}$ (96), no repeat in width

This fine rococo design was produced for an American customer and is likely to have been taken from a "document" in America, since none is known in England. The original was probably printed in blue, hence the title. The sample in the "Machine-book" for 1950–51 (1651M) is printed in purple.

Baker Record Sample A4761

34 BIRDS AND FRUIT, plate-printed cotton
English; Nixon & Co.; about 1770
54 × 34 (137.2 × 86.3) REPEAT: $37\frac{1}{4}$ (94.6), plate wider than textile.

Birds, including two magnificent peacocks, are plate-printed in red on a white ground. There is a paper impression for this design numbered "87" in the Nixon pattern-book (cat. 33). One of several designs with peacocks of the time, usually depicted on a grand scale.

Bakers block-printed part of the design in 1913 as "Boscobel" design no. P56, and screen-printed it in 1964, design no. R9401.
Exhib: English Chintz, 1960, cat. 78
Lit: Montgomery, *Printed Textiles*, 1970, p.232 and fig. 217.

V&A Circ. 11-1956 Given by G.P. & J. Baker Ltd. (illus. p.33)

35 Block-printed fustian
English or French; 1770–75
44 × 32 (111.7 × 81.3) REPEAT: $15\frac{3}{4} \times 10\frac{1}{4}$ (40 × 26)

The cotton has a white ground, block-printed with flowers in the "Indian" taste in black, three tones of red, two purples, dull yellow and pencilled blue.

Bakers printed this design by copper roller in 1924 ref. no. x6565.
Exhib: Farnham 1982 C5 p.24 and pl. VI

Baker No. I004

H1709
Jameson & Banks
H 1709

36 Plate printed cotton
Probably English 1770s
33 × 37½ (83.8 × 95.2) (both max.)
Plate: The full height and width of the cotton

Arborescent design printed in madder red with additional pencilled blue, pink and yellow (the latter now faded). The rendering of this design may be compared with similar block-printed designs such as cat. 37. Other pieces of the design survive in Colonial Williamsburg and Toronto.

Bakers screen-printed the adapted design in 1971 as "Floral Bough", (B416). It is still available.

Baker No. H002

37 Block-printed cotton
French; last quarter 18th century
42 × 35 (100.8 × 89.9)
Block H. 37 (94) W. width of material

Arborescent pattern with exotic flowers in purple, red, pink, blue, yellow and buff and combinations of these colours with a black outline. The treatment of this design may be compared with cat. 36 which is plate-printed. Such designs became part of the traditional *repertoire* of the calico-printer.

Bakers screen-printed the design in 1966 as "Clive" (B357) and again in 1983–84.

Baker No. G048

38 The TURF INN, plate-printed cotton
English; 1780–90
52¾ × 30 (134 × 76.2). REPEAT H. 31 (78.7) W. wider than textile.

The cotton is printed in red with a race taking place outside the Inn. There are versions in black and sepia. A very popular chintz for versions survive in several collections including the V&A (Circ. 104-1960). One version has the monogram "BF" on the back of the carriage, probably the initials of the designer or manufacturer.

Bakers screen-printed the design in light and dark brown in 1973 as "The Turf Inn" (A0792) and it is still in production.
Lit: Montgomery *Printed Textiles* fig. 270 and p.260; *English Chintz* cat. no. 158

Baker No. A126

OVERLEAF *(p.48)* 76 *Design by G. Meynier for the centre of a shawl, printed by Swaisland for Jameson & Banks, 1851–2.*

(p.49) LEFT 77 *Design for a shawl by G. Meynier, Paris, for Swaisland, 1851–2.*
RIGHT 75 *Design for a shawl, for printing by Swaisland, 1849.*

39 CHINOISERIE, plate-printed cotton
French (Jouy); 1785–90
54½ × 26½ (max.) (138.4 × 67.3) REPEAT: 41 × 33¾ (104.1 × 85.7)

The cotton is printed in red with motifs taken from different pattern-books. Similar vases of flowers occur in A. Fraisse *Livre des Desseins Chinois*, 1735. A fragment with the factory's stamp has survived and there is a cotton with the complete height in the Cleveland Museum of Art, 40.39.

Baker No. U191

40 PATTERN-BOOK of original designs for 'Small Chintz & Dress', 1770s to early 19th century
18½ × 14 (47 × 35.5)

G.P. Baker labelled this book: "Much of great interest. Pillement originals . . . from which many good things may be produced". It contains nearly all 18th-century designs, mostly large scale floral trails of the 1770s and 1780s, including these fantastic flowers of the kind seen in Jean Pillement's *Fleurs de Fantasie dans le goût chinois* and *Fleurs de Caprice*, both published in London in 1760. A few kerchief borders are on paper watermarked 1803–08. One design has the pencilled name "Charles Swaisland, Crayford", and it is likely that the book at one time belonged to his collection of old designs kept for the inspiration of his designers.

Baker Collection

41 PATTERN-BOOK "Small Chintz & Dress" designs, late 1780s to 1790s
Printer at Mitcham, Surrey ?
20 × 14 (50.8 × 35.5)

This book, in which G.P. Baker noted "2 colour small effects for Viyella and No. 24", contains designs for many small-patterned dress materials, mainly the dark grounds, with some dove-colour, yellow and black, noted as fashionable in O'Brien's *Callico Printer's Assistant* of 1792. Many of the patterns imitated the striped woven silks of the 1790s. Near the bottom of the right-hand page shown, in two colourways, are simple triangular leaves, the designs for Barbara Johnson's "callicoe gown" of May 1792 (V&A T.219-1973). One pattern with its number and client's initials corresponds exactly with one in V&A loan 3, which contains orders to Howard & Co. (1803) and Howard, Rivers & Co., Mitcham, Surrey (1808).

Baker Collection. V&A loan 6

42 Original design, gouache and watercolour on paper
French, Mulhouse; about 1780–95
$10\frac{1}{4} \times 8\frac{1}{2}$ (26 × 21.6)

Delicately painted on a black ground with wild roses, alpine strawberries, convolvulus and other flowers in brown, orange, yellow, cream, green, blue, mauve and pink. The irregular shape would disguise the repeat when the blocks were cut. Chintzes with very dark grounds and neat, accurate flowers are typical of the late 18th century.

Bakers printed the design by copper roller in 1925 (when dark grounds were again very fashionable) (x6701).

Baker No.25626M (illus. p.37)

41

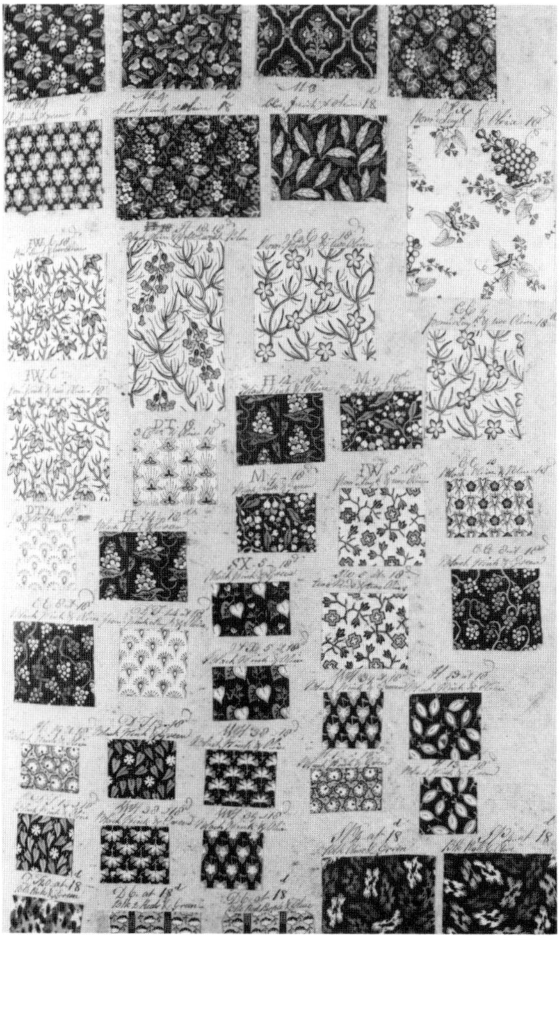

43 Block-printed cotton
French (Mulhouse?); late 18th century
15 × 16 (38.1 × 40.6) REPEAT: $8\frac{5}{8} \times 6\frac{3}{4}$ (21.9 × 17.1)

Black ground with the pattern reserved and then block-printed in blue, yellow, green, two shades of red, and pale olive, with neatly defined flowers. Many such patterns were printed in Mulhouse and in England from the late 1780s to the mid 1790s.

Bakers printed the design in 1931 by copper roller (reference 2419) as "Wyburd Chintz" (F551).

Baker No. H301

44 BODICE, block-printed cotton
French; c.1790
20 × 30 (50.8 × 76.2) REPEAT: $8\frac{3}{8} \times 7\frac{1}{8}$ (21.3 × 18.1)

The cotton has a brownish red ground with naturalistically drawn flowers in two pinks, blue, yellow, green and reserved in white. It is lined with white linen.

Baker No. K008

45 Headscarf; cotton block-printed border
French (Alsace); about 1780–90
37 × 38 (94 × 96.5)

Triangular block with a floral group in the corner.

The border is block-printed in two pinks, blue, yellow and combinations of these with a black outline with delicate, naturalistic flowers and sea-weed. The slightly smudged corner of the block would not show when the scarf was tied.

Bakers printed the design by copper roller in 1960 (reference 3316), called "Ramms Rose Stripe".

Baker No. H367

46 BORDER, block-printed cotton
French (Mulhouse); about 1790
$8 \times 39\frac{3}{4}$ (20.3 × 100.9) REPEAT: $8 \times 18\frac{3}{16}$ (20.3 × 46.2)

The cotton is finely printed with a horizontal border of classical decoration surmounted by a frieze of naturally drawn flowers including a passion-flower and a carnation on a dark ground with sea-weed fronds.

Bakers printed the design as an allover pattern by copper roller in 1931 (reference 2451) as "Fern Chintz from Border" (F583) and by screen in 1981 as "Maywood" for export only. No. B0570.

Baker No. H266 (illus. p.40)

ABOVE 91 *Block-printed linen c.1897, design based on Turkish and Persian cut velvets.*
RIGHT 82 NEW PEACOCK, *block-printed glazed cotton. Drawn by R. Christie 1893–4.*

48

LEFT *Block-impression Mulhouse, late 18th century.*

47 **WOMAN'S JACKET, two cottons lined with fustian**
Late 18th century
H. $29\frac{1}{2}$ (74.9) REPEATS: incomplete

The jacket is made partly from Indian cotton painted in red and partly from cotton plate-printed in red. The latter was printed at Bromley Hall c.1780. (Plate-impressions in the V&A E.458(98, 99)-1955, P.14 "Talwin and Foster 8d".) The jacket is lined throughout with red checked fustian (two versions) made up from seventy pieces.
Exhib: Farnham, 1982, A11
Lit: Montgomery, *Printed Textiles*, 1970, fig. 246, pl. XXVIII (blue)

Baker No. Y022

48 **CHINOISERIE, block-printed cotton**
French (Mulhouse); late 18th century
32 × 38 (81.3 × 96.5)

White ground printed in primary colours with a balloon staffed by *chinoiserie* Chinamen cheered on its way by a *chinoiserie* crowd below, presumably another reference to the ascent of Montgolfier's balloon, see cat. 49. A block-impression of the balloon appears in Vol. 152 p.38 in the Musée de l'Impression, Mulhouse, possibly designed by Haury (?)

Bakers screen-printed the design in 1983 (A0989) see cat. 246.

Baker No. U250

49 **VALANCE, block-printed linen**
French; 1785–1800
11 × 50 (27.8 × 157.5) REPEAT: outer block $6\frac{1}{2} \times 18\frac{1}{4}$ (16.5 × 46.3); inner block $4 \times 8\frac{1}{2}$ (10.2 × 21.6)

Coarse linen, resist printed by block in indigo with a different pattern on each face of the linen.

The outside celebrates Montgolfier's balloon ascent of 1783, a theme for much popular art. The inside has a vertical floral stripe. The whole is bound with a narrow silk ribbon. Two printings of the resist and then dipping in indigo were necessary. This was a typical country furnishing and even dress fabric of the late 18th and early 19th century.

Baker No. W003

50 **PASSION-FLOWER, block-printed cotton**
English; Bannister Hall for Richard Ovey, 1802
32 × 20 (81.3 × 50.8) REPEAT: $15\frac{1}{2} \times 17\frac{5}{8}$ (39.4 × 44.7)

A large passion-flower printed in red, yellow, buff, black and pencilled blue with part of the flower

50

reserved in white. The leaves are green made by an unfaded combination of blue and yellow. There are three blue warp threads in the selvage to denote its English origin. The original design belonging to Stead McAlpin is inscribed on the back "No 105. The Scarlet ground white passion flower chintz R. Ovey 10th December 1802".
Exhib: *English Chintz*, 1960, cat. 195
Lit: *British Textile Design*, Tokyo, 1980, vol. II, pl. 282

V&A Circ. 334-1955 Given by G.P. & J. Baker Ltd.

51 **PATTERN-BOOK, original designs for furnishing, 1803–04**
Vint & Gilling, Crayford? (Vint & Dixon, 1804)
19 × $12\frac{1}{2}$ (48.2 × 31.2)

The most striking designs in this book are the group of drab style demi-chintzes, floral and pillar prints. The design on the right is inscribed on the back:

ABOVE *(top)* 93 TULIP TREE, *block-printed wool, C.F.A. Voysey 1893.* *(below)* 98b SALANUM, *screen-printed cotton 1978, drawn by Ann Lynch from the Voysey design* LEMON TREE.

CENTRE 99 CHATSWORTH, *block-printed cotton and linen fancy cloth, C.F.A. Voysey c.1897.*
FAR RIGHT 96 *Watercolour design for printed linen, C.F.A. Voysey c.1893.*

"D. Goddard. O2. Wild Cherry blossom engaged to Mr. Ovey by Mr. Gilling". The other design, from O1, was also for Richard Ovey, a leading London linen-draper called "Furniture Printer" though other firms did his printing. The pillar print was probably also by Daniel Goddard, having the characteristic thick black line making a cast shadow to one side of the design. Another signed Goddard in V&A loan 7, and designs in loans 7 and 8 marked Vint & Co. have, with "Mr. Gilling", led to the attribution of these three books of furniture designs to Vint & Gilling, Crayford (see page 29)
Exhib: English Chintz, 1960, cat. 214
Lit: Peter Floud, *The Drab Style and the Designs of Daniel Goddard*, *The Connoisseur* cxxxix, 1957, pp.234–239

Baker Collection: V&A loan 9

52 Roller-printed cotton
English; 1810–20
43 × 25 (109.2 × 63.5) REPEAT: $20\frac{5}{8} \times 23\frac{1}{2}$ (52.4 × 59.7)

An open window with carefully draped curtains looks out on to a garden with a Grecian Temple in the distance and a couple strolling by a lake. The cotton is printed in red with additional yellow and buff added by surface roller. Ackerman's Repository illustrated such curtain drapes from 1811 onwards. Registration mark on selvage.

Bakers reproduced the design by copper roller in 1930 and 1938, (F406 and F845), and screen-printed it in 1963, (B340) always as "Open Window". The 1938 and 1963 versions show the totally different effect achieved by the change in colours and techniques for both are accurate reproductions.
Lit: Montgomery, *Printed Textiles*, pp.76–77

Baker No. J025 (illus. p.41)

53 DUDDING'S FURNITURES, pattern-book of block-impressions on paper, c.1815–20
$21\frac{1}{2} \times 37$ (54.5 × 94)

The stationer's label dates the purchase of the empty book to 1811–20. Another label states that G. Oakley (in London Directories 1807–26, and possibly the Oakley of Oakley, Dudding & Co., Furniture Printers, 1802–05) has purchased all the printing blocks and patterns of Mr Dudding (Dudding & Nelson, 1806–10, E.B. Dudding 1811–16) "designed by Artists of Celebrity and peculiarly adapted to Rooms of every Class, with appropriate Taste". The V&A has another book with this label (T.86-1964) full of borders in the Egyptian, Indian, Chinese, Pompeian and Neo-classical tastes. The volume displayed contains some of these, but mostly fillings including several imitating large-scale silk damask

51

51

52

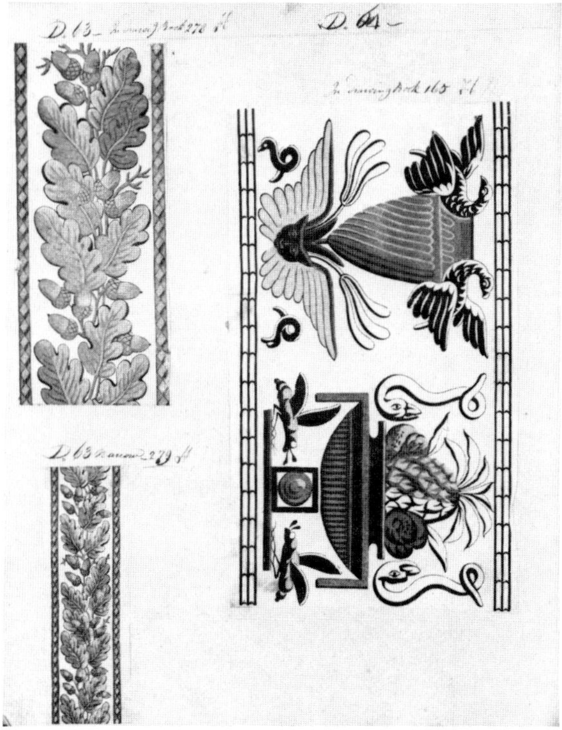

53

OVERLEAF *(left)* 102
LYNHAM, *design in watercolour and body colour for textile, Silver Studio 1898. (right)* 106
Watercolour design for printed linen, Harry Napper 1907.

patterns. Baker Tuckers owned the Oakley/Duddings book, and original Duddings designs can be found in their scrapbooks 2 and 3 (cat. nos 26, 81).

Baker Collection. Ex-Baker Tuckers

54 Block-printed cotton

English; about 1815–20
$24\frac{1}{8} \times 59\frac{1}{2}$ (61.3 × 151.1) REPEAT: 16 × 13 (half drop) (46 × 33)

Tea ground with pattern areas reserved in white, printed with a partridge under a palm tree in red, yellow, light purple, pink, blue and combinations of these. Variations on the theme of partridges or other birds and palm trees on tea grounds were popular for ten or fifteen years.

Bakers block-printed the design in 1908/9, block C286 (P345) as "Partridge" and printed it by copper roller, reference 3324 in 1926 (X664) and 1937 (F806).

Baker No. H200 (illus. p.40)

55 PRINCESS CHARLOTTE, block-printed cotton border

English; about 1816–17
$24\frac{1}{2} \times 6\frac{1}{16}$ (62.2 × 15.4)

Vertical border with classical decoration and a miniature containing a portrait of Princess Charlotte (1796–1817) married 1816, in buff, red, blue, yellow, pink and combinations of these colours. A horizontal version of the border appears in Hunton *English Decorative Textiles*, 1930, fig. 112.

Baker No. U190

56 THE FARMYARD, plate-printed cotton handkerchief

English; 1820–40
43 × 41 (109.2 × 104.1)

The handkerchief is printed in purple with a few block-printed details in red. It was originally printed on fustian by John Collins, Woolmers, Herts. in 1765 and later by Nixon & Co., Phippsbridge, Surrey. There are pieces of the 18th-century version in the V&A (T.443-1919), Boston, the Metropolitan Museum of Art and Winterthur. The added border dates the handkerchief.

Bakers reproduced it in 1951 by copper roller (reference 3107) as "Farmyard" (A454) and again by screen in 1983–84.
Lit: Montgomery, *Printed Textiles*, fig. 254 & p.255; *English Chintz*, cat.82.

Baker No. A100

57 Block-printed cotton
English; Bannister Hall; 1825
$15\frac{1}{4} \times 16\frac{1}{4}$ (39.4 × 41.9) REPEAT: incomplete

A border of wider and narrower floral stripes in madder colours with pencilled blue on a light tea ground.

Bakers printed the design by copper-roller in 1927 (reference 2078) as "Blue Edged Chintz" (F306) and screen-printed it in 1979 as "Mrs. Fitzherbert's Stripe" (A913), from their own historic fabric of this design, H276.

Exhib: Cotton Board, 1955, no. 125
English Chintz, 1960, no. 313

V&A Circ. 368-1960 Given by G.P. & J. Baker Ltd.

58 HYDRANGEA, roller-printed cotton
English; 1825–30
$47 \times 24\frac{3}{4}$ (109.3 × 62.8) REPEAT: $25\frac{5}{8} \times 9\frac{5}{8}$ (65.1 × 24.5)

Hydrangeas and other flowers roller-printed in red on a dark tea ground with blue and yellow added by surface roller. Bakers retain a piece of this fabric H199.

V&A Circ. 365-1960 Given by G.P. & J. Baker Ltd.

59 Roller-printed cotton
French; Mulhouse?; about 1830
25 × 24 (63.5 × 61) REPEAT: $12 \times 13\frac{1}{2}$ (30.5 × 34.3) half drop

Columns with classical capitals at intervals alternate with sprays of flowers, in purple and red with blue and yellow added by block or pencilling. Columns were very fashionable motifs both in France and England at the time and there are many block impressions in Mulhouse for similar textiles. Bakers retain a piece of the fabric, H035.

V&A Circ. 391-1960 Given by G.P. & J. Baker Ltd.

60 Roller-printed cotton
English; about 1830
$45\frac{3}{4} \times 23$ (116.2 × 58.4) REPEAT: $18 \times 12\frac{1}{2}$ (45.7 × 31.8) half drop

Blue ground roller-printed in red, the yellow added by surface roller. The ever-quickening need to produce new designs and a wider, less discriminating market resulted in a deterioration in styles long before the mid 19th century. Bakers retain a piece of this fabric, H116.

V&A Circ. 13-1956 Given by G.P. & J. Baker Ltd.

61 Roller-printed cotton
English; about 1830–40
66 × 54 (167.6 × 137.2) REPEAT: $15\frac{5}{8} \times 12\frac{3}{4}$ (39.7 × 32.4) half drop

Glazed cotton with vertical stripes in a textured effect contrasting with bunches of flowers between – a passion-flower, rose, hops, etc. – in pink, blue, orange and brown, and combinations of these colours. The design shows the influence of the botanical works of the time.

Bakers printed the design by copper-roller (2988) in 1940 as "Pin Stripe" (A296), and screen-printed it as "Filigree Stripe" in 1978 (A0848).

Baker No. Y124

62 FISH BOWL, roller-printed cotton
French or English; about 1830–40
23.5 × 30 (59.7 × 76.2) REPEAT: H. $18\frac{1}{4}$ (46.4) W. wider than the textile.

A pattern in pink of goldfish bowls nestling among flowers with an inquisitive bird perched on the rim. The bowls differ slightly on each side.

The design was printed by copper roller (2369) by Bakers in 1930 as a glazed polychrome chintz (F528). The fish in the bowls have been swapped in the reproduction.

Baker No. A048

63 FERN TRAIL, roller-printed cotton, 1932
$54 \times 31\frac{1}{2}$ (137.2 × 80) REPEAT: 15 × 15 (38.1 × 38.1)

This exquisite colourway could be taken for an original of the early 19th century, but for its shade of single green. The ground almost covered with ferns and flowers is similar in style to designs in V&A loan 9, cat. 51, and to the fern design in cat. 64. Sample 2513, in a different colourway, in one of the copper-roller books, is dated April 1932, with the inscription: 'Used for 840 SK on 17/1/39'.

Baker Record Sample A692

64 Roller-printed cotton
Probably French; 1835–45
$29\frac{1}{4} \times 24\frac{1}{2}$ (74.3 × 62.2) REPEAT: $17\frac{1}{16} \times 15\frac{5}{8}$ (43.3 × 39.7)

The cotton is totally covered by ferns, roses and other flowers in red and yellow (now faded).

Bakers printed the design by copper roller, (2468) as "Fern Bouquet", (F524) in 1931 and again in 1954, copper roller reference 3151 (B200). The meticulous Studio drawing of 1931 (8732M) $19\frac{1}{4} \times 14\frac{5}{8}$ (48.9 × 37.2) shows the polychrome design giving a three-dimensional effect.

Baker No. H025 (illus. p.40)

65

67 and 67a

65 LIME STREET STATION, LIVERPOOL, block-printed cotton
English; 1836–40
$37\frac{3}{4} \times 26\frac{1}{2}$ (96 × 67.3) REPEAT: $25\frac{1}{2} \times 12$ (65 × 30.5)

The cotton has two views, of the outside and inside of the station, with a side border showing Euston Arch (built 1836, demolished 1965). Liverpool's station, opened in September 1830, was the first to take passenger traffic. The new terminus at Lime Street was opened in 1836. The main features of the cotton are in black with a sepia wash. The decoration of the station arch is in red, yellow, blue and green. (Lilac may have faded to become indistinguishable from sepia.) The trains are cursorily drawn – the Rocket is not even on the rails.

Baker No. U226

66 FALSE PRINCIPLES IN DESIGN NO. 11, DIRECT IMITATION OF NATURE, block-printed chintz
English or French; mid 19th century
$51\frac{3}{8} \times 52$ (130.5 × 132.1) REPEAT: $31\frac{3}{4} \times 25\frac{1}{2}$
(80.6 × 64.7) approximately half drop

Brown ground block-printed in green, blue, mauve, red, pink, cream and buff with life-size sprays of lilac and roses. J.U. Tournier designed this fabric for Schwartz-Huguenin of Alsace 1840–45 but it seems to have been speedily copied in England. The Department of Practical Art held an exhibition in 1852 of "False Principles in Design". A group of the fabrics shown was given to the South Kensington Museum, probably by the 1851 Exhibition Commissioners, and it included this design later registered as T.10-1933. Whatever critics thought the design has been in production virtually ever since.

Bakers screen-printed the design in 1967 on linen (R862) and on glazed cotton for F. Schumacher & Co.
Lit: Tuchscherer, 1972, fig. 109

Baker No. F997

67 STAFFORDSHIRE DOGS, roller- and surface-printed cotton, c.1850
English; probably printed in Lancashire
$29\frac{1}{2} \times 32$ (75 × 81.2) REPEAT: $13\frac{1}{2} \times 32$ (34.2 × 81.2)

This typical mid-Victorian design, of dogs with a dead hare in a landscape set in a wreath of flowers, was used at least twice by Bakers. Among the firm's newspaper clippings is a cutting from the *Evening News* of August 5th, 1925 illustrating this subject, from W.H. Haynes' Collection purchased in California, with the comment: 'A choice design copied from an old document. It is a favourite with

104 HEMLOCK, *design in body colour for printed textile, Harry Napper 1899.*

owners of hunting and shooting boxes.' Made for that market, the sample in Bakers' copper-roller book dated 22/9/25 shows the dogs still with the dead hare, unlike the 1976 version displayed here, cat. 67a.

Baker No. H384

67a STAFFORDSHIRE DOGS, screen-printed cotton, 1976
$35\frac{1}{2} \times 54$ (90.2×137.5) REPEAT: $24\frac{3}{4}$ (63), half-drop in width of material, with dogs in reverse.

The design of Document H.384 is here adapted to 54 inch from 36 inch material, and the dead hare has been omitted. This design is still in production.

Baker Record Sample B0490

68 Roller-printed cotton
American; 1848–50
$21 \times 24\frac{1}{2}$ (53.3×62.2) REPEAT: H. $13\frac{3}{4}$ (34.9), W. wider than textile

The cotton is printed in shades of brown and green with a battle scene commemorating the capture of General la Viga by Captain May, and other scenes from the battle of Resaca de la Palma in the war between the United States and Mexico.

Bakers printed the scene in 1949 and 1957 by copper roller, reference 3051 called "Battle Scene" (B41).
Lit: Montgomery, *Printed Textiles*, fig. 409 p.344

Baker No. H038

69 THE GREAT EXHIBITION 1851, roller-printed cotton
English; 1851
32×28 (81.3×71) REPEAT: $14\frac{5}{8} \times 28$ (37×71)

The cotton is printed in light green, dark green, blue, maroon, olive and brown. The pattern is taken from one of the many popular prints of the time. The V&A possesses a handkerchief (T.87-1961) and another piece of the same textile, (T.12-1951).

Bakers reproduced the design by copper roller in 1931, reference 2319 called "Crystal Palace" (F482).

Baker No. H231

70 PAGE FROM COPPER-ROLLER BOOK, 1923
Bakers' printed sample after a late 1830s design
$12\frac{1}{2} \times 9$ (31.7×22.8)

The pattern shows part of a stylised bird. It was adapted, in reverse and with minor alterations, from an engraving of a shawl called "The Bird", made in Teheran, published in an album for the use of French shawl manufacturers, which is believed to have appeared in 1837 (*Le Cachemirien*, ed. Fleury Chavant, Paris, n.d.). That this pattern was produced by G.P. & J. Baker is important for the history of English shawl manufacture, for Bakers are most likely to have had the design among their vast collection of Swaisland patterns, evidence for the latter using French printed sources of design.

Baker copper-roller sample 1884.

71 DESIGN FOR PRINTED DRESS FABRIC, watercolour on paper, 1845
For printing by Charles Swaisland, Crayford
8×8 (23×23)

This undated design is taken out of Swaisland book 18, where there is also a similar design that was registered as printed dress material by Charles and Amos Swaisland on February 1st, 1845. Similar designs survive in other Swaisland design books, including a very fine one in a volume marked "French Drawings". Swaisland sample books of Spring 1845 to Spring 1846 (V&A loan 21, 22) contain pages of more simplified stripe and wave patterns with rich shaded colours. About twenty years later, Swaisland's used the design displayed here without its shaded stripe to form wide borders for a printed handkerchief, possibly for Joseph Oxford & Co. (V&A loan 35). The timeless quality of the design led to G.P. & J. Baker producing it at least twice, in 1896 (Block-book, B393) and 1934 (Block-book, D5).

Baker Collection (Removed from a pattern-book.)

71

72 GLAZED CHINTZ FROM A SHAWL DESIGN, 1909
G.P. & J. Baker, after a Swaisland original c.1843–44
18 × 24 (45.7 × 60.9) REPEAT 4½ × 4 (11.4 × 10.2)

The shawl pine design is similar to several in the Swaisland design books for 1843–44; but it has not yet been found in an exact equivalent. In the original it is likely to have been one element in a more complicated design, as in cat. nos 75, and 75a. The chintz is dated by the design in Block-book no. C282.

Baker Record Sample X154

73 DESIGN FOR A PRINTED SHAWL, watercolour on paper, c.1843–47
For printing by Charles Swaisland, Crayford
26 × 21½ (66 × 54.6)

Colouring and pattern suggest the above date; but the equivalent has not yet been identified in any Swaisland design book or in the Representations of Registered Designs. Possibly it was a design which did not go into production, as unfortunately happened at first with the projected Baker version, cat. 73a.

Baker Collection. Unbound design no. 29

73a CASHMIR SQUARE, design intended for a screen-printed cotton, watercolour on paper, 1964.
Adapted by Ann Lynch for Bakers
19 × 16¾ (48.2 × 41.2)

Drawn for a 50″ screen-print (SC3064) from the original design for a Swaisland block-printed shawl, cat. 73, this design was not used in 1964. It may be produced, in 140 cm width, for the 1984–85 range.

Baker Collection P2784.

74 BOOK OF SKETCHES FOR PRINTED FABRICS, c.1845–47
Shawl border designed by G. Haité for Swaisland
18 × 11 (45.7 × 28)

G.P. Baker wrote: "Much of the work in this book is Chas. Hudson & George Haité, 1845 & 1849 . . . of exceptional merit!". Rough covers bound towards the middle of the book are inscribed "C. Hudson 1847" and "G. Haité 1847". Some designs are dated 1845. Pagination and paper changes do not aid identification of individual designs. The line drawings in ink of naturalistic floral borders for handkerchiefs are probably the work of Hudson. Some of the shawl designs and repeating patterns are analogous to designs by Haité given to the V&A by his son (Department of Prints & Drawings).

Baker Collection (one sketch illus. p.48)

75 DESIGN FOR A PRINTED SHAWL, watercolour on paper, 1849
Charles Swaisland, engaged to Keith & Shoobridge
45 × 16 (114.3 × 40.6)

Keith & Shoobridge, described in commercial directories as "shawl printers", had their printing done by Swaisland and by Glen & McIndoe of Glasgow. The latter won a prize medal for their "economical execution" of the firm's shawls in the Exhibition of 1851: but it was one of their Swaisland shawls that was depicted in the Art Journal Illustrated Catalogue of the Exhibition (p.308). This earlier design, Swaisland's numbers H1370, 1371, dated September 15th 1849, was not registered.

Baker Collection. Unbound design no. 77 (illus. p.49)

75a SWAISLAND PINE, screen-printed cotton, 1967–68
Adapted by Ann Lynch from a shawl border design
17 × 51½ (43.2 × 130.8)

The pine and stripe were taken from a design for a shawl border which Charles Swaisland engaged to Keith & Shoobridge in 1849 (cat. 75). This printed cotton did not go into production.

Baker No. Sc.2966

76 ORIGINAL DESIGNS FOR PRINTED SHAWLS, 1851–52
Designed by G. Meynier for printing by Charles Swaisland, engaged to Jameson & Banks
20½ × 14 (52.1 × 35.5)

Swaisland's "F&H" book for shawls and dress c.1851–55 shows here designs registered (84319, 84328) on 22nd March 1852. H1709, inscribed "Jameson & Banks", is only the centre of the shawl, the Representation in B.T.43.175 revealing an elaborate pine border, in all over five feet deep. Three designs in exactly this style engaged to the same firm in 1851 (V&A loan 26) have the stamp of G. Meynier of Paris (see cat. 77). The commission agents Jameson & Banks won Honourable Mention in the 1851 Exhibition for "superior shawls . . . printed by the first men in the art such as Swaisland, Littler and David Evans".

Baker Collection (one design illus. p.45)

77 DESIGN FOR A PRINTED SHAWL, watercolour on paper, c.1851–52
Designed by G. Meynier for Charles Swaisland
41¼ × 15½ (104.8 × 39.3)

This fantastic design is undated and does not appear to have been registered. Possibly it was considered too bold and not produced. Designs incorporating trees and rustic fences were popular in the years

1851–52. In the Swaisland "F&H" books and among the unbound designs for shawls are a few with the stamp of G. Meynier, 1 Rue d'Hauteville, Paris, with that firm's running number. No. 327 is on a design for Jameson & Banks of 1851 (V&A loan 26): this is no. 549. G. Meynier *Frères* won an Honourable Mention for shawl designs in the Paris Exhibition of 1855, with commendation for their uses of photography.

Baker Collection, Unbound design No. 2 (illus. p.49)

78 BLOCK-PRINTED WOOL SHAWL, 1859
Charles Swaisland for David Evans & Co.
137 × 71 (348 × 180.5) REPEAT: $11\frac{1}{2} \times 8\frac{1}{2}$ (28.5 × 21.7)

Sewn to this shawl is a label with the name of David Evans, the silk and shawl printers of Crayford, celebrating the First Class Medal awarded to Swaisland shawls in the Paris Exhibition of 1855, and stamped with the Registered Design mark for February 5th, 1859 (no. 118368 is the filling, B.T.43.178). Border, filling and edging designs are stuck pages apart in V&A loan 29, one inscribed "D. Evans". Patterns created from tiny pink and orange flowers massed on blue and green foliage were in vogue though the late 1850s and early 1860s, many of the finest being made by Swaisland for Evans. The filling pattern was later used by Swaisland's Printing Co. Ltd. for a handkerchief (P11435).

Lent by Martin Baker (detail, illus. p.28)

79 BLOCK-PRINTED SCARF, 1947
G.P. & J. Baker, from a Swaisland's design
$34\frac{1}{2} \times 34\frac{1}{2}$ (87.6 × 87.6)

The pattern corresponds to Block-book No. D517, which is inscribed "5 Blocks. Old F.6073". This shows the use in 1947 of an old Swaisland's design, which, from its "Filling" number, originated in 1869.

Lent by Martin Baker

80 PATTERN-BOOK OF DESIGNS, 1860–86
Pages shown, Swaisland's Printing Co. Ltd., 1870
11 × 14 (27.9 × 35.5)

These designs for a tablecover and "Paisley" handkerchief borders, registered by Swaisland's on October 15th and 18th, 1870, occur also in the Cutting Department Register from 1870 (V&A loan 39). Designs for the "Paisleys" dated August 1st and 8th, 1870 are in "Swaisland Hkfs" (V&A loan 35). Their appearance as completed handkerchiefs, with additional "Paisley" fillings and plain red edges, can be seen where two of these designs recur, as N9641H and N9666F, in another, undated, book of handkerchief designs. The volume on display covers the early 1860s to 1886, including printed ribbons shown at the 1862 Exhibition (for Cox & Co., Franklin & Son, Cornell & Co.), handkerchief borders (mainly for J. Oxford & Co., R. Curwen & Co.), tablecovers and even slipper-fronts.

Baker Collection

81 PATTERN-BOOK, "BAKER TUCKERS NO. 3"
Designs for their own handkerchiefs, c.1840s
20 × 14 (50.8 × 35.5)

G.P. Baker summed up as "an odd lot of stuff" this scrapbook miscellany of engravings from books, a few 18th- and many 19th-century paper-impressions and designs, including some original designs for Dudding's borders (cat. 53), and printed cotton samples in harsh reds, browns and blues, besides many designs for Baker Tuckers' own production of printed corahs and bandana handkerchiefs. A few of these designs, with stylised and semi-naturalistic floral motifs, are inscribed "Rangoon" with dates in 1870, and "For Messrs Baker Tuckers & Co.".

Baker Collection

The Swaisland Printing Works, Crayford in Kent.

G.P. & J. Baker – the first twenty years

THE POPULARITY OF EASTERN CARPETS and embroideries had already been proved to the Baker firm, and as early as 1877 they decided to explore the possibility of having textiles made in England patterned with these designs. George Percival Baker, on behalf of his father, approached a number of manufacturers asking their terms to copy, as printed textiles, a selection of embroideries which had been imported by the Company from Turkey and neighbouring countries.[1] Only one reply has survived, from Thomas Wardle of the Hencroft Works in Leek, Staffordshire.[2] Wardle, now well-known in his own right and as the printer of William Morris's early textiles, was not keen to undertake unrenumerative trials for Bakers without some guarantee of being engaged "with some degree of permanency". This work, which Wardle described as "to design or copy Persian and other eastern ornament for printing" was very similar to the type of work being done by Wardle at the time, his own designs showing the influence of his own travels in India and the Near East and often printed on to imported silks. Wardle invited Baker to send a few of the "old pieces" to him for consideration. As he intended to use vegetable dyes in the trials,[3] it is probable that his estimated prices were too high, and the offer was not taken up. The letter book 1886–88 shows that a number of printing firms had been used by the Bakers, none of whom proved entirely satisfactory. Instead G.P. Baker turned to the Swaisland Printing Company in Crayford, Kent, first heard of through Minnie Baker's father, Robert Davis, at that time auditor to the firm. From 1870 the company had been owned by a limited liability company under the chairmanship of Henry Honey whose son was manager of the works.

It is not clear when Swaislands first produced printed textiles for Bakers. Pattern books from the print works are not helpful as they show many textiles based on eastern designs made for different clients, the fashion for such patterns having first been made popular by Liberty & Co. and printed for them by Thomas Wardle. Printing was under way, however, by 1887 when Jim Baker and Percy Pulman joined G.P. in London, before Jim wrote to his father "Your gold printing – we are trying experiments at Swaislands. I will send you samples as they turn it out" in October 1888.

Expansion at Ivy Lane had seen the formation of three sections dealing with carpets, textiles and export goods of various kinds. At an early stage Jim took charge of the carpet section with G.P. involving himself in the development of the textile section. Whereas he clearly saw himself as an independent trader, his father George saw both sons as still part of his own empire and it is his letter, of April 4th 1892 (already mentioned) which finally broke this bond. Referring to his "London business" in carpets, he set out his last balance sheet up to July 29th. "From that date I will give you each 5,500 pounds with goodwill fixtures . . . to trade on your own account."

The *Furniture and Decoration* magazine for February 1st 1893 heralded the start of the new company with the announcement "Mr G.P. Baker, Turkey Carpet Manufacturer & c., of 16 Ivy Lane, has admitted his brother Mr. Jas. Baker into partnership. The new firm will be known as Messrs. G.P. & J. Baker." The first directors of the new company were G.P. and James Baker, Percy Pulman and Charles Percival and, appearing in trade directories for 1893, the Company was listed as trading in three separate areas:

1. Importers from Turkey, Persia and India and wholesale merchants of Oriental Carpets.
2. Producers and Dealers in Art Printed Fabrics.
3. Commission Agents involved in buying and selling from Eastern firms.

Swaisland Printing Works

In 1891 the Swaisland Printing Company went into voluntary liquidation. Printed textiles had, by this date, become an important part of the firm's trade and G.P. suggested to Jim "that there was nothing for it but to become printers ourselves, and that any loss we might sustain I personally would bear".[4]

By 1893 G.P. Baker was negotiating with the owners of the Footscray Printing Works when one of the Swaisland liquidators approached him and offered the Swaisland Bleach Works (known as the "Lower Factory")[5] at a rental of £135 per annum with an option to buy within two years at fourteen years rental. The Works were visited and a lease was signed on April 4th 1893 between G.P. Baker and the liquidators, Henry Honey and Alfred Blow. This included "Factory, Warehouse, Boilerhouse, Chimney, Reservoir, Well, Dam, Pool, Sleuces, Tumblers, Water, Implements, Fixtures, Cottages, Land Rights, Easements, appurtenances etc.". At the same time the "Upper Factory" was bought by the firm of Messrs Bowran and converted into a Tannery. Many of the young men employed by the Swaisland Printing Company had, by 1893, moved to Lancashire to work in the printing trade there, but G.P. Baker re-employed those that were still in the Crayford area[6] including John Doyle, who had been in charge of the Block Printing Section. As the majority of Bakers' early textiles were block-printed, Doyle became Manager of the Works and advised G.P. on the sale of equipment from the "Upper Factory". Much of the printing equipment from the Bleach Works had been sold to France in the 1870s so he must have welcomed the opportunity to buy printing tables, printing and washing machines and a large number of printing blocks (mostly of "cashmere" designs) at knock down prices. The catalogue,[7] with annotations in Doyle's handwriting, is still in the possession of the Baker family.

G.P. Baker bought the Printing Works within the two year limit, and in turn leased it to G.P. & J. Baker, the firm, with an option to buy. This was done in 1907 at a cost of £4,000.

Being importers of oriental carpets, the partners conceived the idea, on first taking possession of the Works, of hand-knotting rugs to their own chosen designs. Upright looms were set up alongside the printing tables and this work was carried out by girls using wools dyed in the factory.

As expected, the first full year at Crayford was not profitable but by 1896, with the installation of a ten-colour printing machine, the Firm's success was assured. Unfortunately the production of carpets was sacrificed for this increase in orders, and the looms were dismantled to make room for the installation of more printing equipment.

In 1904 John Doyle retired and was replaced by Harold Clayton, who had trained and worked in the Lancashire printing industry.[8] He remained with the Firm until his retirement in 1948.

In 1894 the Company's London showrooms were moved to 3–9 Warwick Square and a little later they acquired an outlet in Phoenix Court, New Gate Street. Carpets were displayed in Phoenix Court, under the management of Percy Pulman. The textile department was, under Charles Percival, in a wing of the main building. A designer called Fletcher was employed and a Mr Akers took charge of exports and shipping to Constantinople. Minnie Baker's father also joined the Firm as accountant. An archive of historical textiles had been started with pattern books acquired from the Crayford Works and this was added to by G.P. Baker and Charles Percival on their business trips to Europe and America. This was the general organisation of the Firm up to 1907 when the carpet section was transferred to a separate company, O.C.M. under the direction of Jim Baker.

G.P. & J. Baker flourished, and profits for the year 1902–6 showed an average of £11,312 12s 3d with stock in trade on July 30th 1906 (including the Freehold and equipment of the Crayford Works and the leasehold of the London premises) calculated at £67,812 15s. In April 1907 the Firm went public "for the purpose of paying off existing charges and loans and adjusting various family interests and also because the expansion of the business renders the introduction of further capital desirable". All debts were paid (including the purchase of the Crayford Works) and Percy Pulman and Charles Percival were repaid for earlier financial investments with 200 ordinary shares plus the balance in cash. As Directors they were also put under contract for seven years to act as Managers for the Firm.[9] On May 10th 1907 G.P. & J. Baker commenced business as a limited company.

Baker Textiles: Stylistic Developments 1893–1914

The Firm's surviving pattern books of block-printed textiles for this period provide a fascinating summary of fashionable furnishing textiles, including as they do the work of other retailers printed at the Swaisland Works. Although owned by Bakers, the Print Works' records were kept separately and Bakers' own designs are represented by a code (no. 10) as with other companies involved. Few of these firms can be positively identified today. Only one, Liberty & Co., can be identified by code (no. 24) although it is known from labels and other marks on existing samples that prints were also made for Story & Co. and Heal & Sons at the Swaisland Works. These represent only a small proportion of clients, however, as up to 1905, Bakers' own work provided only 60 per cent of the Print Works' orders. It is very likely that many firms, previously employing the Swaisland Printing Company to print for them, kept their work with the factory after the change of ownership.

Only eight of G.P. & J. Baker's textile designs were registered with the Patent Office and all these registrations occurred between March 1893 and February 1894.[10] This would suggest that the Firm was anxious to announce its arrival to competitors rather than protect any of its designs.

The Drawing Room at Mr and Mrs G.P. Baker's home "Ivydene" in Bexley, where they lived until 1926. Turkish and other eastern textiles and tiles can be seen.

Nothing is known about the Firm's first designer, identified by G.P. Baker simply as "Fletcher", although he could have been F.W.H. Fletcher who is known to have designed naturalistic floral wallpaper designs for Jeffrey & Co, in 1880.[11] It is likely that early traditional reproduction designs, such as "Pelargonium" (cat. 84) and others (cat. nos. 83, 85) were drawn by Fletcher from historic samples and designs with such names as "Jonquil", "Primula", "Old Rose Chintz", "Hybiscus" and "Hydrangea" all suggest that the sources of the designs were mid 19th-century printed textiles.

Turkish Influence

The influence of Turkey and the East is strongly marked on textile designs printed from 1893 (cat. nos. 86 to 92A) and a contemporary photograph of Greek and Turkish embroideries in G.P. Baker's home shows the source of such designs. "Bokhara", "Brusa", "Caldium", "Zaprak" and "Syrian Curtain" are all copied from imported embroideries or carpets, much of the so-called "gold work" already referred to, and a number of original western designs bought at the time also bear eastern names. A bias towards traditional patterns – pomegranates, palmettes and artichokes in particular, can also be seen in early prints, and examples such as "Scutari" (cat. 87), which was drawn at least four years before it was printed, show that these designs were selected from designers' work rather than commissioned especially. A number of Bakers' eastern patterns were also adapted for other manufacturers (cat. nos. 88, 90).

Free-lance Designers

Between 1893 and 1914 fifty-seven different designers are listed as supplying designs to Bakers. As it is known that the Firm's design studio had no more than two staff throughout this period one must assume that most work was bought from free-lance artists. Many names appear over and over again in the Firm's records. Not only the famous are listed and many designers are unknown apart from single designs they sold to Bakers. In line with contemporary manufacturers and retailers, however, the most successful designs were produced by a small number including such eminent names as C.F.A. Voysey, Lindsay P. Butterfield, Harry Napper and Charles Haité. In patronising such designers, Bakers are likely to have been influenced particularly by the shop Liberty & Co., whose development, in the types of textiles that they sold, parallels Bakers' own. Throughout the 1880s and 1890s Liberty's held exhibitions of historic and contemporary eastern embroideries, and began to sell Thomas Wardle's eastern-inspired printed velvets and silks as early as 1880. By 1896 they were buying a number of textiles from Bakers as well as having a number of their own designs printed at Crayford.

The Print Works had produced velveteens before Bakers took over, and velveteen tablecloths 36 inches (91.5 cm) square became some of their most popular lines, many of which were sold by Liberty's at 5s 6d each. Although a number of designs for these, by Voysey and Butterfield still exist,[12] only one incomplete sample is known. Showing a Voysey design of tulips, this is now in the collection of the Württembergisches Landesmuseum, Stuttgart.[13]

The most prolific textile designer of the late 19th century was C.F.A. Voysey and this exhibition shows only a small selection of his work for Bakers. It does, however, show all aspects of his versatile talents, from early traditional patterns (cat. nos. 87, 89) to florals in the style of William Morris (cat. 93) and from whimsical figurative panels (cat. nos. 94, 95) to his characteristic bird and flower designs (cat. nos. 96 to 100) for which he is now best known.

The designs of Lindsay Butterfield and Charles Haité were well matched to G.P. Baker's own interests, both specialising in beautifully drawn, delicately stylised designs of garden flowers. More designs by these two artists were used by Bakers than those of any other artists between 1900 and 1905. It is probably their work above all others printed by the Firm which helped to develop a characteristic style for the period. Both Voysey and Butterfield sold the same design to more than one client, and a number of Bakers' printed designs can also be found as woven wool, silk and gauze fabrics produced by Alexander Morton of Darvel, Scotland.[14]

A watercolour by Ernest Skinner of one of G.P. Baker's own hybrid iris. Ernest Skinner was, for a time, in charge of the Firm's design studio.

Exclusive copyright was bought with designs from the Silver Studios, however, and archives at Middlesex Polytechnic give dates and prices for each bought. Arthur Silver's view that "There are manufacturers and manufacturers; generally speaking, the majority want good art which will also show a profitable return, and they ought to have it" (*Studio* III, 1894) was well met by G.P. & J. Baker and their business with Silver Studio shows an appreciation of original contemporary design at its finest (cat. nos 101 to 103). This unfailing interest is shown by the fact that the Firm continued to buy designs from Harry Napper, one of the most original designers of his time, after he left the Silver Studio (cat. nos 104 to 106).

Of the lesser known designers employed in the early 20th century rather obvious choices were made with the purchase of designs by Sidney Mawson and Allan Vigers, whose specialisation in naturalistic floral designs follow the Firm's development closely. Less understandable is the use of Cecil Millar's designs, which border on geometry and abstraction. Their marked debt to peasant art, however, was at the very core of the Firm's foundation.

Art Nouveau Designs

The English evolution of this style is quite different to that seen on the Continent and the eccentric swirls and distorted forms seen in French and Belgian textiles held no attraction for British manufacturers. Instead, a general stylisation of floral forms was developed. In Bakers' textiles for the period, designs show flat, often white grounds many, surprisingly, with traditional ogee or trailing repeat motifs, and designs by Butterfield and Napper show exaggerated, elongated flowerheads drawn in bright colours with an economy of line (cat. nos. 117 to 121). Unlike other manufacturers, Bakers did not indulge in the full extravagances of the *art nouveau* movement and even their choice of designs from Harry Napper (the British designer most influenced by continental work) show his least eccentric patterns. Bakers' textiles, however, were sold by the most fashionable shops in Europe and found their way into many foreign homes and Museum collections.

Stylised Floral Designs

The most popular designs printed by Bakers from the mid 1890s to 1910 show naturalistically drawn English garden flowers and fruit and the development of this style is their trade-mark today. Early examples show a stylisation in the positioning of leaves and stems around flowers, in very simple yet pleasing repeating patterns with pure flat colours often outlined with black. Sometimes a deliberate stencilled effect with shaded colours can be seen (cat. nos. 107, 121, 130, 131, 143) which enriches the overall effect. Flowers chosen also follow the current fashion in gardening with emphasis on trailing plants and those often used in herbaceous borders. Tulips, roses, geraniums, ivy, tiger lilies, fritilleries, pinks, vetches, marguerites and climbing alpine plants are all represented in these designs (cat. nos. 122 to 132). By 1903 names of designs also followed fashion, in common with other manufacturers, and instead of bearing the name of the plants from which they were taken, place names became popular.

Copper Roller Printing

Although it is known that a ten-colour printing machine was installed at Crayford in 1896, few early textiles other than block-printed samples, can be found outside the Firm's first machine pattern book (cat. 137). Examples in this book confirm that designs were similar to those used for block-printing, and at least one block pattern, "Ryde" (cat. 145) was also printed by engraved roller. As with the Firm's block-printed products, a number of machine-printed textiles were sold through Liberty's including three examples exhibited (cat. nos. 139 to 141). A few figurative designs were also sold through this shop including "The Cinderella" which was sold for nursery curtains and covers[15] and a set of nursery cushions, designs for two of which are also exhibited (cat. nos. 135, 136). Scenes depicting characters in Dutch costume were particularly popular and were first used in nursery wallpapers and friezes designed by William Kidd and Cecil Aldin.[16] The cushions were available "in a variety of rich and harmonious shades" in cotton at 1s 9d and velveteen at 2s 11d.

The Early Twentieth Century; Modern Traits in Design

Throughout the various stylistic stages described, it must be remembered that G.P. & J. Baker had always produced a concurrent range of high-quality reproduction textiles and although few appeared in the period 1896 to 1905, it is interesting to note that more were introduced into the Firm's range at a time when strenuous efforts were being made to introduce modern styles. Designs by Pattison and Burn (cat. nos. 146, 147), a number of which appeared in *The Studio Year Books* for 1906 to 1908, show a more modern adaptation of the traditional floral forms for which the Company is now well known. Denser in detail and heavier in line and colour, these show a transitionary period in the history of design from natural to abstract form.

The influence of work produced at the Glasgow School of Art is also evident in Bakers' designs; "Square Rose" (cat. 150) and "Jewel Tree" (cat. 151) in particular show the favoured Scottish motif of isolated, stylised roses. "Saltash" (cat. 152) shows a similar approach with alternating blocks of floral details, and the tendency towards small, isolated tree-like forms, popular from 1902–4, can be seen in cat. nos. 148 and 149.

A predilection for small repeating patterns continued to be popular and, as a reaction from the large-scale complicated floral designs of the 19th century, geometric patterns became fashionable. Woven textiles and carpets produced at the Wiener Werkstätte in Austria had a dramatic effect on the design of furnishing fabrics and their simplicity, using natural yarns and colours, was widely emulated. Bakers were brave to buy such *avant garde* designs, however, so different from their normal range. Of the four examples shown (cat. nos. 153 to 156) only one (cat. 153) has a design derived from curving forms; the others are purely geometric. "Siebers", listed as the source of these designs, cannot be traced in Austria today, so it is not known whether this refers to a designer, studio, or agent.

It is unlikely that any of these Viennese designs were best sellers and the Firm was never again to favour non-floral designs. From this time their range concentrated on both newly drawn traditional floral designs (cat. nos. 157, 158, 161) and adaptations of historic samples (cat. 159) both very popular with the interior design trade then as they are now. Occasional original designs of woodland and garden scenes appeared (cat. 160) in keeping with an interest in landscape gardening by the Baker family and the general public. It was the first twenty years of production which proved G.P. & J. Baker as successful manufacturers of fine quality furnishings and this was achieved with the insight and imagination of the founders and those who worked for them.

LINDA PARRY

84

87

Bakers' records identify designers by their surnames only; further information is given wherever possible.

82 NEW PEACOCK, block-printed glazed cotton, 1893–94
Drawn by R. Christie from a 19th-century textile. Sold through Heal & Sons
39 × 31 (99 × 78.5) REPEAT: 30⅞ × 31 (79 × 78.5)

Stylised peacocks with fanciful jewelled tails sit on mossy branches with brown birds in flight, bamboo leaves and blossom in yellows, greens, red, blue, black and other colours on a white ground.

One of Bakers' most popular designs which has been revived since Christie's drawing. Known to the firm as "Christie's Bird". Heal & Sons catalogue c.1915 illustrates this textile with a purple ground called "Chinese Peacock".

Block B13. Baker Record Sample F241 (illus. p.53)

82a Block-printed cotton, second half 19th century
English, printed with turkey red dyes
34¾ × 23½ (89 × 60) REPEAT: 23 × 23½ (89 × 60)

Original cotton from which the above was drawn. On a red ground, the colours are less vivid than in Christie's adaptation.

Baker No. H238

83 Block-printed glazed cotton, 1894–95
"Reproduction" design
43 × 25½ (110 × 65) REPEAT: 27¾ × 21¾ (71 × 56)

A floral trail design showing flowers, including wild roses, carnations, hyacinths and stocks, growing from a common stem. In shades of red, pink, blue and green on a white ground.

One of a series of naturalistic floral designs printed by Bakers soon after the Firm was established showing a style which was to become their trademark in the 20th century. Probably adapted from an early 19th-century design.

Baker Record Sample F3

84 PELARGONIUM, block-printed glazed cotton, 1895
"Reproduction" design
34 × 25½ (87 × 65) REPEAT: 17¾ × 25½ (45.5 × 65)

A naturalistic design of trailing pelargonium plants in shades of yellow, pink, maroon and green on a white ground. Adapted from an early 19th-century design. Block B103, printed with twenty blocks.

Baker Record Sample F1/2

85 Block-printed glazed cotton, c.1895
"Reproduction" design
35 × 25½ (89 × 65) REPEAT: 10 × 8⅓ (26 × 21.5)

Floral spray design of wild flowers, including

cranesbill, deadly nightshade and cats ears in pinks, reds, blues, yellow and brown with purple and black stems and outlines on a white ground. Adapted from an early 19th-century design.

Baker Record Sample X126

86 PATTERN BOOK of block-printed impressions for textiles, from 1893
$27\frac{1}{2} \times 17\frac{1}{2}$ (70.5 × 44.5)

Containing small samples, mostly of paper showing impressions from Bakers' range of block-prints from 1893 when they took over the Swaisland Works. Samples displayed show early items of Turkish influenced designs, a few of which were registered with the Patent Office (see separate entries).

Baker Collection

87 SCUTARI, block-printed linen, 1893
Designed by C.F.A. Voysey
$38\frac{1}{2} \times 26\frac{1}{2}$ (99 × 68) REPEAT: $24\frac{3}{4} \times 9\frac{3}{4}$ (62 × 25)

Rows of traditional pineapple motifs in shades of green.

The design was registered by Bakers on November 22nd, 1893 together with two other Voysey designs of Turkish influence. The original design, which is owned by Bakers is inscribed "for velvet", and was drawn before 1890. Block B15, printed with five blocks.

Baker Record Sample P172/1 (illus. p.77)

88 Block-printed cotton, 1893–1900
Printed for Heal & Sons
$51\frac{1}{2} \times 33$ (130 × 84) REPEAT: $10 \times 4\frac{1}{4}$ (25.5 × 11)

Cone motifs comprising small floral sprigs in green, yellow and pink on a white ground.

"Heal & Sons" is printed along the selvage. An early design printed by Bakers for this illustrious firm. Few other examples of this association can be traced.

Baker Record Sample P76/2

89 Block-printed cotton and linen slub ground, 1893–1900
Possibly designed by C.F.A. Voysey.
$53\frac{1}{2} \times 36\frac{1}{2}$ (136 × 93) REPEAT: 16 × 12 (41 × 30.5)

Traditional artichoke design of repeating ogee motifs with surmounted crowns at intersections. In green, yellow, purple and white on a red ground.

Similar in style and drawing to other early Voysey designs. A very similar textile design was registered by Liberty in 1893 and it is possible that this textile was sold through this establishment.

Baker Record Sample P35/4

90 THE ANATOLIA, copper roller-printed linen, c.1905
Reproduction design, sold through Liberty & Co.
$11\frac{1}{3} \times 7\frac{3}{8}$ (29 × 19) REPEAT: not shown

Stylised floral design on a natural linen ground in blue, olive, dark pink and dark yellow with some outlining and cross-hatching in black.

One of Bakers earliest designs taken from their collection of Turkish embroideries. Originally block-printed (Block C285) this design was adapted at a later date for Liberty and sold by them at 2/11d a yard. The original design is owned by Bakers.

V&A T.351-1976 Given by Liberty & Co.

91 Block-printed linen, c.1897
Reproduction design
$16 \times 32\frac{1}{2}$ (42 × 83) REPEAT: $7 \times 3\frac{1}{2}$ (18 × 9)

Traditional repeating design of palmettes in dark pinky red with yellow and green foliage and black outlines on a white ground.

Based on the patterns of Persian and Turkish cut velvets of the 16th and 17th centuries, this design may have been drawn in the Baker studio from the original sample of velvet. The design is owned by Bakers. Block C63, printed with four blocks.

Baker Record Sample P174/2 (illus. p.52)

92 FAWLEY, block-printed linen, 1903
Designed by G.C. Haité.
34 × 31 (87 × 79.5) REPEAT: $2\frac{3}{4} \times 3\frac{3}{4}$ (7 × 9.5)

Vertically striped design of stemmed pointed palmettes in two shades of blue on a white ground.

Manufactured at the height of Bakers' production of *art nouveau* designs this, and the following adaptation, show the Firm's lasting interest in Turkish designs. The original design, on tracing paper, is owned by Bakers. Block B944, printed with two blocks.

Baker Record Sample P112/1

92a EGMONT, block-printed linen, 1903
Designed by G.C. Haité.
34 × 31 (87 × 78) REPEAT: $7\frac{1}{4} \times 3\frac{3}{4}$ (18.5 × 9.5)

Vertically striped design of stemmed palmettes with divisions in green every third row. Palmettes in red and green on a white ground.

An adaptation of FAWLEY. According to Bakers' block book both printed in "April 1903". Block B945, printed with two blocks.

Baker Record Sample P113/2

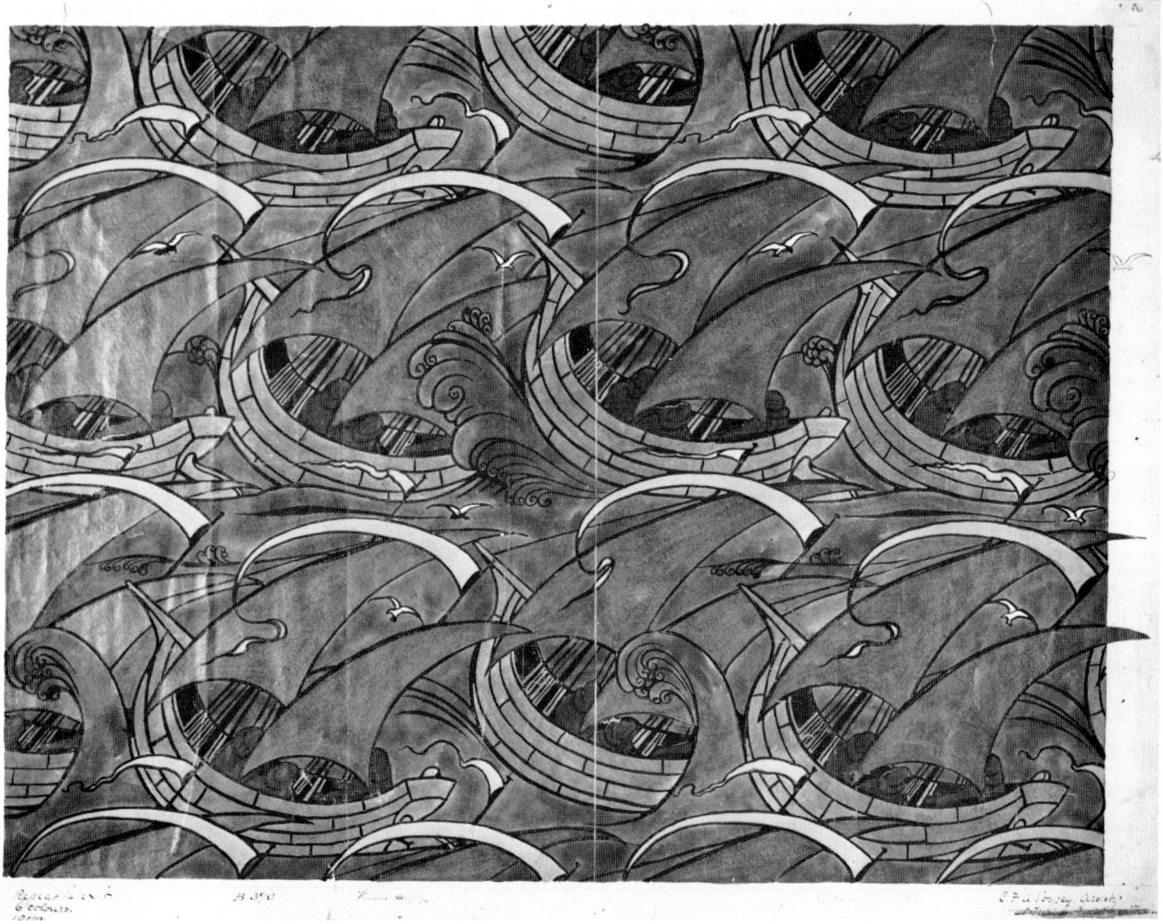

95

97

CHARLES FREDERICK ANNESLEY VOYSEY (1857–1941)

Trained as an architect by J.P. Seddon, Saxon Snell and George Devey and set up his own practice in 1882. Started to design wallpapers and textiles under the guidance of his friend A.H. Mackmurdo and from 1884 sold wallpaper designs to a number of companies. The most prolific and original textile designer of the 19th century he sold designs to nineteen manufacturers producing woven and printed textiles and carpets. His influence was great in Britain and on the continent and his name became associated with the European *art nouveau* school after one of his wallpapers was used in Henri Van de Velde's first famous *art nouveau* building the Tassel House, in Brussels.

His designs for Bakers are particularly interesting spanning a wide range of styles from early pre-1890 patterns of eastern influence to his more characteristic designs of people, animals and flowers in broad, flat colour in obvious designing motifs.

93 TULIP TREE, block-printed wool, 1893

Designed by C.F.A. Voysey, sold through Story & Co.
19 × 27¾ (48 × 70.5) REPEAT: 14¾ × 11¾ (37.5 × 30)

Stylised branching blossoms of tulip-shaped flowers arranged in horizontal rows with meandering stems and haphazard leaves. In shades of green, yellow, grey and peach with black outlines on a cream ground, the design has a small subsidiary design in brown.

Registered by Bakers on November 8th, 1893, the first Bakers design printed at Swaislands. A label attached to this sample reads "Story & Co. Art Fabrics, 49 & 51 Kensington High Street, London W". It was sold on a wide woollen twill ground (60 inches) at 5/11d per yard. No cotton samples of this design have been found. Block B3, printed with seven blocks.
Exhib: Cotton Board 1955, 255 (cat. p.48)

V&A T.25-1953 Given by C. Cowles Voysey (illus. p.56)

94 COLUMBUS or SHIP, block-printed linen, 1894

Designed by C.F.A. Voysey.
16 × 32¾ (41 × 84) REPEAT: 13⅞ × 10 (35.5 × 26)

Repeating design of sailing ships with open sails being rowed by six sailors. Horizontal bands of ships are alternated with lighter stripes representing a stormy sea with birds in flight. In shades of blue with black outlines.

Noted in the block book as "purchased thro Drew". As there are no records to suggest that Voysey dealt directly with Bakers, this is possibly the name of the agent or block-cutter involved. Block B19.

Baker Record Sample P305/1

95 THREE MEN OF GOTHAM, design for a printed velveteen, body colour and ink on paper, watermarked 1889

Designed by C.F.A. Voysey, Printed by G.P. & J. Baker 1894
21½ × 28⅜ (55.5 × 72.5) REPEAT: 14½ × 15 (37 × 38.5)

A repeating design of three men in a boat tossed on a stormy sea in shades of blue, green, red, orange and yellow.

An article in the *Studio* magazine for 1893 (p.236) describes this design as being still in Voysey's possession. As it is signed with Voysey's Streatham address, it must have been drawn before 1890 when he moved house. One of a series of designs depicting boats produced by the firm throughout the 19th and 20th centuries. Block B390, printed with six blocks.
Exhib: Voysey, 1978, D47 (cat. p.119)
Lit: *RIBA*, Symonds, fig. 93 *(illus. p.72)*

Lent by the British Architectural Library (RIBA 659)

96 Design for a printed textile, watercolour and body colour on paper, c.1893

Designed by C.F.A. Voysey
25⅛ × 16⅝ (64 × 42) REPEAT: 15½ × 10½ (40 × 27)

Long-necked birds, perched on stems with large blue flowers, peer to left and right through scrolling acanthus leaves. In orange, yellow, blue and shades of green on a dark blue ground.

A border design of the same birds and scrolling leaves in the Baker Collection was probably drawn as a border, to be used as a printed velveteen tablecloth. The same elongated bird motif appears in other Voysey designs for this period.

V&A E.59-1961 Given by G.P. & J. Baker Ltd. (illus. p.57)

96a Block-printed linen, c.1900

Designed by C.F.A. Voysey and Printed for Liberty & Co.
52 × 32¼ (133 × 81) REPEAT: 15½ × 10¼ (40 × 26)

Textile printed from the above design. In shades of green and yellow on a natural linen ground.

Bakers' toning down of the original vivid colourings are in keeping with fashion for 1900, some years after the design was drawn. Printed as a "Liberty Art Fabric".
Exhib: Liberty's 1975, D35 (cat. p.48); Voysey 1978, D23 (cat. p.107).

V&A T.62-1953 Given by C. Cowles Voysey

108 HONESTY, *water-colour design for printed textile: C.C. Haité 1896.*

97 Block-printed cotton velveteen, c.1895
Designed by C.F.A. Voysey, probably sold through Liberty & Co.
89½ × 32 (229 × 83.5) REPEAT: 18¾ × 11 (48 × 28)

Meandering design of gourd-like plants showing fruit and flowers in yellow, green and brown on a greeny-brown ground.

Woven in 1898 as a muslin by Alexander Morton & Co. and called "Aspidistra". Originally designed as a printed tablecloth; the block book refers to "4 borders, 4 corners, 3 fillings". A very similar design, with the gourds opened out and printed on to a coarse linen is in the V&A collection (Circ. 237-1966). This sample bought in Brussels at the end of the 19th century. Block B808, printed with eight blocks.
Lit: V&E.D.A. 1952, S27t (cat. p.103) (muslin) *Dekorative Kunst*, Vol. 1, 1897–8, p.269. Tilliet, fig. 25, pp.210–11

Lent by the Musées Royaux d'Art et d'Histoire, Brussels (TX1251) (illus. p.79)

98 LEMON TREE or LEMON BLOSSOM, design for a printed textile, watercolour on paper, 1896
Designed by C.F.A. Voysey
22 × 16 (56.5 × 41)

Diagonal trails of lemon blossom showing fruit and flowers. In lemon yellow, greens and blues on a white ground.

Inscribed with the artist's name and Carlton Hill address and the date February 20th, 1896. There is a design in the V&A for the same textile given by G.P. & J. Baker (E.63-1961). Of similar colouring the ground is dark terra-cotta and an inscription reads "Lemon Tree – Design for a tablecloth". A border design for this is in the Baker Collection.

Baker Collection

98a LEMON TREE or LEMON BLOSSOM, block-printed cotton velveteen, 1896
Designed by C.F.A. Voysey
10½ × 12 (27 × 31) REPEAT: not available

Small sample of the original velvet from the above design. In pinks and greens on a spotted orange ground.

Designed originally for velveteen, with or without a border, this design is referred to as "Lemon Blossom" in the block book. Block B389, printed with six blocks (including one optional ground blotch).

Baker Collection

98b SALANUM, screen-printed cotton, 1978
Drawn by Ann Lynch from the original Voysey design
38½ × 54¾ (98.3 × 140) REPEAT: 17½ × 8¾ (45 × 22.5)

Design as above. Shades of green, pink, grey and brown on a pale lime green ground.

Re-issued to coincide with the Voysey exhibition at Brighton, Ann Lynch studied all original existing samples and colourings in preparing this design. In the Bakers' range for 1978 and 1979.

Baker Record Sample A0900 (illus. p.56)

99 CHATSWORTH, block-printed cotton and linen fancy cloth, c.1897
Designed by C.F.A. Voysey. Sold through Liberty & Co.
50½ × 59½ (129 × 152.5) REPEAT: 14¾ × 10½ (37.5 × 26.5)

From vertically curving stems grow pods, tulip-shaped flowers and exotic leaves. In shades of yellow, grey and green with white outlines on a dark pinkish maroon ground.

Produced as "The Nure" wallpaper by Essex & Co., and as a leno by Alexander Morton & Co. Designs for ground and border in the Baker Collection. Block B510, 9 blocks for textile, twenty-one with borders.
Exhib: Cotton Board, 1955, 258 (cat. p.48). English Chintz 1960, 443 (cat. p.66).
Lit: *Studio*, XVIII, 1900 p.48 (illus. as wallpaper), *Der Moderne Stil* 2, 1900, no. 3, taf. 90.

V&A T.61-1953 Given by G.P. & J. Baker Ltd. (illus. p.56)

99a CHATSWORTH, block-printed cotton velveteen, c.1897
Designed by C.F.A. Voysey. Sold through Liberty & Co.
19 × 13 (48.5 × 33.5) REPEAT: 14¾ × 10½ (38 × 27)

Design as above, in shades of green and white.

A popular design on the continent, this sample was bought in Liberty's shop in Paris in 1914, another example is in Stuttgart Museum (GT6401).
Lit: Tilliet, fig. 23, p.208. Stuttgart, 1980, no. 47, p.73

Lent by the Musées Royaux d'Art et d'Histoire, Brussels (TX953)

100 Design for a printed textile, watercolour and pencil on paper, c.1905
Designed by C.F.A. Voysey
21 × 14¾ (54 × 38)

Unfinished design of birds in foliage in dark green on a white ground.

Baker Collection

100a Block-printed linen, c.1905
Designed by C.F.A. Voysey
35¾ × 32¼ (91.5 × 82.5) REPEAT: 19 × 7½ (48.5 × 19)

Design as above. Stencil-effect shading on birds from lime green to olive, with green leaves and black outlines on a natural linen ground. Block C224, printed with three blocks.
Exhib: Voysey, 1978, D25 (cat. p.108, illus. 109)

V&A T.63-1953 Given by C. Cowles Voysey

100b HEDGEROW, screen-printed cotton, 1979
Drawn by Ann Lynch from original Voysey design
34 × 31 (86.5 × 78.5) REPEAT: 7½ × 17½ (19.5 × 45)

Design as above. Olive green, grey and shades of brown on a pale lime ground.

This design was re-issued by Bakers in 1979 and is still in their range.

Baker Record Sample A0901

SILVER STUDIO
Established in 1880 by Arthur Silver (1852–1896). Produced repeating designs for textiles, wallpapers, carpets and wall stencils. These were sold to all the leading manufacturers and agents of the day and their designs can be seen in the work of Liberty, Alexander Morton, David Barbour, Warners, Newman, Smith & Newman, F. Steiner & Co. and both the Swaisland Printing Company (up to 1891) and the later G.P. & J. Baker. On the death of Arthur Silver the studio was continued by his son Rex, with Harry Napper directing the fabric and wallpaper side of the business. Other designers known to have worked for the Studio include John Illingworth Kay (who sold free-lance designs to Bakers), Stacy Aumonier and J.R. Houghton, chief designer from 1898–1901.

In 1967 the collections of unsold designs and archives of the Studio was given by Mary Peerless, step-daughter of Rex Silver, to Middlesex Polytechnic; see *The Silver Studio Collection*, London, 1980.

101 THISTLE, block-printed cotton velveteen, 1896
Silver Studio Design no. 1749. Probably sold through Liberty & Co.
28¾ × 32½ (73.5 × 83.5) REPEAT: 23½ × 29¼ (60 × 75)

A design of thistles and yarrow in shades of green, beige, mauve, brown and white on a sky-blue ground.

Two designs (one for a border) are in the Baker Collection. The design was purchased from the Silver Studio in November 1896 for 9 guineas. This sample was bought from Walther, Frankfurt-am-Main in 1912. There are other samples of this design in public collections including a sample of woven cotton at the V&A (Circ. 261-1966). Block B432.
Lit: Stuttgart 1980, 14, pp.39, 42. Tilliet fig. 21 pp.204, 5.

Brussels, Musées Royaux d'Art et d'Histoire (TX981)

102 LYNHAM, design for a printed textile, watercolour and body colour on paper, 1898
Silver Studio Design no. 1913
27¼ × 21½ (70 × 54.5)

Swirling leaves and tulip heads on a swirling striped ground. In shades of pink, green, cream and yellow on a blue ground.

Design bought from Silver Studio in March 1898 for £5 15s 6d. Block B553, printed with eight blocks.

Baker Collection (illus. p.60)

103 CONVOLVULUS AND SEEDPOD or TOADSTOOL, block-printed cotton velveteen, 1898
Silver Studio design no. 1910. Textile sold through Liberty & Co.
29½ × 22¾ (75.5 × 58.7) REPEAT: 17¼ × 29¼ (44 × 75)

Design of scrolling acanthus leaves and flowers in shades of green, blue, white, violet and yellow with black outlines on a blue ground.

The design was bought from the Silver Studio in March 1898 for 8 guineas when it was called "crocket scroll". This piece bought from Walther, Frankfurt-am-Main in 1912. A sample in the V&A is printed on a cotton and linen ground (T.53-1953) and is on permanent display in the Museum. This sample was exhibited at the exhibitions listed below. Block B588, printed with thirty-four blocks.
Exhib: Cotton Board 1955, 262 (cat. p.49); English Chintz 1960, 450 (cat. p.67); Libertys 1975, D32 (cat. p.49)
Lit: Liberty trade catalogue *Liberty Tentures* p.16 called "Thistle"; Tilliet, 18, pp.200, 201

Lent by the Musées Royaux d'Art et d'Histoire, Brussels (TX951)

HARRY NAPPER (died 1930)
Joined the Silver Studio in 1893 and in 1896 took over from Arthur Silver in managing the section dealing with repeating designs. After 1898 he worked as a free-lance designer occasionally selling designs through the Silver Studio. A watercolour artist and

LEFT 130 *Block-printed linen, G.C. Haité c.1900*
ABOVE 111a APPLE, *block-printed linen, L.P. Butterfield c.1898.*
RIGHT 116 PANSY, *block-printed linen, Cecil Millar 1903.*

designer of wallpapers, carpets, woven and printed textiles, embroidery, furniture, metalwork and stencilled wall-coverings, his style was strongly influenced by continental *art nouveau* and subsequently very popular in Europe. Many of the most famous Silver Studio designs are his work (including two of the three shown here).

104 HEMLOCK, design for a printed cotton, body colour on paper, c.1900
Designed by Harry Napper, 1899
$24\frac{7}{8} \times 35\frac{5}{8}$ (63.5 × 91).

Design of swirling thistles and cow parsley in shades of blue, green, yellow, grey and brown on a dark green ground.

The first design sold by Napper to Bakers after he left the Silver Studio. It is likely, from the colouring, that the design was printed on velveteen and cotton. Block B708.

V&A E.70-1961 Given by G.P. & J. Baker Ltd. (illus. p.64)

105 TEAZLE, design for a printed fabric, watercolour on paper, 1900
Designed by Harry Napper, 1899
32 × 30 (81 × 76)

Ogee motif comprising a teazle plant with a number of heads. In shades of pink, green, brown and yellow with black outlines on a yellow ground.

Design bought directly from the designer.

V&A E.69-1961 Given by G.P. & J. Baker Ltd.

105a TEAZLE, block-printed cotton velveteen, 1900
Designed by Harry Napper, 1899
$7\frac{3}{4} \times 12\frac{1}{2}$ (20 × 32) REPEAT: not available

Small sample of the above design in pink, beige, brown and shades of green on an olive ground. Block B700, printed with eighteen blocks.

Baker Collection

106 Design for a printed textile, watercolour on paper, 1907
Designed by Harry Napper
$19\frac{3}{4} \times 14\frac{3}{4}$ (50.5 × 38)

Ogee design of large spiky-headed tulips and stylised roses arranged within scrolling acanthus leaves. In shades of pink, green, brown and gold.

Block book gives the date "June 30 '07" as that when the blocks were cut, so the design could date from the previous year. One of Nappers' most extravagant *art nouveau* designs showing the influence that contemporary continental design had on his work.

Baker Collection

106a Block printed linen, 1907
Designed by Harry Napper
26 × 30 (66.5 × 76.5) REPEAT: $17\frac{1}{3} \times 14\frac{3}{4}$ (44.5 × 38)

Design as above in shades of green, brilliant pink, red and brown on a dark blue ground. Block C186.

Baker Record Sample P296/6 (illus. p.61)

105

GEORGE CHARLES HAITÉ (1855–1924)
Son of George Haité, the Paisley textile designer. Designer of fabrics, carpets, wallpapers, woodcarving and reliefs, metalwork, leaded glass and book illustration although his first love was oil and watercolour painting. He came to London in 1873 and from 1883 exhibited at the Royal Academy. In 1898 the *Studio* magazine described him as "an artist whose range is unusually wide and energy extraordinary" listing twenty-two watercolours and oil paintings that he had exhibited in six exhibitions that year, as well as his numerous designs for the decorative arts.

He was, for a number of years, President of the Society of Designers and showed an interest not only in contemporary textiles but in historic aspects of the Industry. His publications include "On the Design and Designers of the Victorian Reign" in *Architectural Review*, Vol. II, 1897.

He supplied designs to a number of textile manufacturers including Warners, A.H. Lee and G.P. & J. Baker and there are many original designs for his work in the Baker Collection. Many other unidentifiable designs in the collection are also probably his work.

107 CROCUS, design for a printed textile, watercolour on paper, 1893
Designed by G.C. Haité
18 × 29¾ (46 × 75.5)

Rows of swaying crocus plants in shaded colours; mauve to pale blue and lemon to bright yellow with shades of green.

The block book calls this "Rainbow Furniture" which may refer to the technique used and finished weight of fabric. There is an unsigned design for this textile in the Patent Office Registers for 1893.

Baker Collection

107a CROCUS, block-printed cotton and linen fancy cloth, 1903
Designed by G.C. Haité
48¼ × 59½ (123.5 × 152.5) REPEAT: 17 × 59½ (43.5 × 152.5)

Design as above in the same colouring.

There is an inexplicable delay in the printing of this design considering Haité's popularity in the 1890s.
Exhib: V&E.D.A. 1952, Y13 (cat. p.137)
Lit: *British Textile Design*, 1980, Vol. III no. 133 (text xxviii) (*illus. p.88*)

V&A T.57-1953 Given by G.P. & J. Baker Ltd.

108 HONESTY, design for a printed textile, unfinished watercolour with body-colour on paper, 1896
Designed by G.C. Haité
30 × 22 (76 × 56)

Stylised, colourful honesty plants grow in seaweed-like formations in shades of green, dark red, dark pink and yellow with purple-blue outlines on an orange ground.

Although not identified as being a Haité design this is so like his other work, both in technique and style, that identification is possible.

Baker Collection

108a HONESTY, block-printed cotton velveteen, 1896
Designed by G.C. Haité
8¼ × 18¾ (21 × 48) REPEAT: not available

Design as above in gold, dark brown, green, and peach on an orange ground.

Blocks were cut for this design at the "end of December 1896". Block B433, printed with five blocks.

Baker Collection (illus. p.81)

109 HARLEY, block-printed linen and cotton fancy cloth, 1896
Designed by G.C. Haité
51¼ × 62 (131 × 158.5) REPEAT: 15 × 15 (38 × 38)

A repeating ogee motif of succulent hyacinth-like petal forms in blue with stem and floral details in yellows, greens and peach.

There is a design for this textile in the Baker Collection. Block B471, printed with eight blocks.
Lit: *British Textile Design* 1980, Vol. III 132 (text xxvii). (*illus. p.89*)

V&A T.56-1953 Given by G.P. & J. Baker Ltd.

LINDSAY P. BUTTERFIELD (1869–1948)
Trained for three years at the National Art Training School in South Kensington 1889–1891, and in 1890 won an "Owen Jones" prize for tile designs. Took premises with Harrison Townsend at 12 New Court and by 1894 had established himself as a free-lance designer, earning an average of £400 per year by 1898. Art theorist and teacher as well as prolific designer of repeating textiles, wallpapers and carpets. Sold designs to, amongst others, Alexander Morton (from 1902 under contract to this firm), Thomas Wardle, Turnbull and Stockdale and Warners. Some of his very beautiful original designs, showing fine draughtsmanship and a knowledge of botany, can be studied in the Victoria and Albert Museum and a number sold to Bakers from the late 1890s, are still in the Firm's collection.

Butterfield was on the Committee of the Society of Designers, wrote a number of articles on the theory of design and from 1917 taught at the Central School of Art and Design, London.

110 Block-printed linen, 1903
Designed by Lindsay P. Butterfield, sold through Liberty & Co.
42 × 50 (106.5 × 127) REPEAT: 14¾ × 10 (37.5 × 25.5)

Large stylised tulip heads arranged alternately in rows with flat serrated leaves. In shades of blue, mauve, green and dark brown. The ground has a small subsidiary design.

Printed with a solid ground from 1904. The original design is in the Baker Collection. Reprinted in the 1970s by Liberty with a brown and orange colouring. Block C33.
Exhib: V&E.D.A. 1952, Y5 (cat. p.136); Cotton Board 1955, 259 (cat. p.48); English Chintz 1960, 445 (cat. 66).
Lit: *British Textile Design* 1980, Vol. III 134 (text p.xxviii). (*illus. p.90*)

V&A T.59-1953 Given by G. P. & J. Baker Ltd.

LEFT 113 ROSE AND ACANTHUS, *block-printed cotton and linen fancy cloth, Sidney Mawson c.1900.*
BELOW 107a CROCUS, *block-printed cotton and linen fancy cloth, G.C. Haité 1896.*
RIGHT 109 HARLEY, *block-printed cotton and linen fancy cloth, G.C. Haité 1896.*

110

118

114

111 APPLE, block-printed linen, c.1898
Designed by Lindsay P. Butterfield
$86\frac{1}{2} \times 31$ (221.5 × 79.5) REPEAT: $10\frac{1}{4} \times 5\frac{1}{8}$ (26 × 13)

Design of apples hanging from vertical branches in shades of blue with a white outline.

Produced as a woven textile by Alexander Morton c.1903. A signed design was given to the V&A by the artist in 1934 (E.5054-1934). Block C37, printed with four blocks.

V&A T.91-1973 Given by Mrs Mary Harrison

111a APPLE, block-printed linen, c.1898
Designed by Lindsay P. Butterfield
$16\frac{1}{2} \times 16\frac{1}{2}$ (42 × 42) REPEAT: $10\frac{1}{4} \times 5\frac{1}{8}$ (26 × 13)

As above with overprinted yellow on apples.

A second design, possibly made in the Baker studio, is in the Baker Collection.

Baker Record Sample P148/3 (illus. p.85 and endpapers)

112 TRILLIUM, block-printed cotton velveteen, 1896
Designed by Lindsay P. Butterfield
$27\frac{1}{3} \times 13\frac{1}{4}$ (70 × 34) REPEAT: $14\frac{3}{4} \times 10$ (38 × 25.5)

Orchid-shaped flowers and bulbs arranged in ogee formation in grey, reds, yellows and whites on a blue-grey ground.

This sample was bought from a leading continental shop Walther, Frankfurt-am-Main in 1913. Block B584.
Lit: *The Artist*, 1900 (p.103); *Der Moderne Stil 3*, 1901, taf. 8 no. 2; Tilliet no. 2 (illus. p.171, text p.172)

Lent by the Musées Royaux d'Art et d'Histoire, Brussels (TX954)

SIDNEY G. MAWSON (working 1882, died 1941)
Landscape painter and lecturer in textile design at the Slade School. Designer of textiles and wallpapers. Mawson had a very wide range of designs and in the 1890s his work is very eclectic, following the fashionable styles of the day by such designers as William Morris and Lewis F. Day. By the 1900s he produced large floral designs with wide repeats, as in the example exhibited.

He sold textile designs to Alexander Morton, Morton Sundour (including their all-time best seller "Pleasaunce"), Turnbull & Stockdale and Warners.

113 ROSE AND ACANTHUS, block-printed cotton and linen fancy cloth, c.1900
Designed by Sidney Mawson
$50 \times 61\frac{1}{2}$ (127 × 155) REPEAT: $29\frac{1}{2} \times 29\frac{1}{2}$ (74 × 74)

Naturalistic scrolling leaf and flower design. In shades of green, yellow and pink on a mid-blue ground.

A design for this textile is in the V&A (E.67-1961). Block B800, printed with eighteen blocks.
Exhib: Cotton Board, 1955, 266 (cat. p.49) (*illus. p.88*)

V&A T.54-1953 Given by G.P. & J. Baker Ltd.

ALLAN F. VIGERS (1858–1921)
Designer of wallpapers, woven and printed textiles, embroidery and furniture. Known more for his numerous wallpaper designs, his work formed the centrepiece of Jeffrey & Co.'s exhibits at the Franco-British Exhibition in 1908 which was awarded the Grand Prix.

He is known to have supplied textile designs to Warners and Alexander Morton & Co. as well as this piece for G.P. & J. Baker. A number of his original designs are in the Victoria and Albert Museum.

114 MALLORY or THE ROSE, design for a printed fabric, water and body colour over pencil, 1901
Designed by Allan Vigers
$26\frac{3}{4} \times 39\frac{3}{4}$ (68 × 101)

A design of roses, violets and other flowers in various colours.

The design is signed and dated with Vigers' Wimbledon address. It is also inscribed with the block colours "2 reds, 3 greens, 1 yellow, 1 purple, 1 blue".
Lit: *Der Moderne Stil*, VI, 1904 (taf. 7, pl. 19)

V&A E.5513-1960 Given by Miss Mary Vigers

114a MALLORY or THE ROSE, block-printed linen, 1902
Designed by Allan Vigers
29 × 31 (73.5 × 78.5) REPEAT: $14\frac{3}{4} \times 31$ (37.5 × 78.5)

As above in shades of pink, mauve, blue and red with dark green outlines on an olive ground.

Also referred to as "Rose and Pansy". Block B813, printed with eighteen blocks.
Exhib: A&C 1903 (155B, 364); V&E.D.A. 1952, Y10 (cat. p.136); Cotton Board 1955, 271 (cat. p.50); English Chintz 1960, 456 (cat. p.68)

V&A T.58-1953 Given by G.P. & J. Baker Ltd.

ABOVE 122a TIGER LILY, *block-printed linen, L.P. Butterfield 1896.*
RIGHT 131a GERANIUM, *block-printed linen, Burnet 1902.*

CECIL MILLAR (active from about 1900)
Designer of wallpapers, textiles and furniture. Described in the 1909 *Studio Year Book* as producing designs for "almost every article necessary for the filling of a house". Particularly successful as a textile designer, he sold a number of designs to Bakers from the early 20th century. His characteristic style is modernistic in approach and often geometric in bright colours, based on the shapes and motifs of peasant and folk decoration.

115 ALBURY, block-printed linen, 1902
Designed by Cecil Millar
46 × 31½ (118 × 81) REPEAT: 11 × 7½ (28 × 19.5)

Ogival design of stylised trees and flowers. In shades of green, pink and yellow on a white ground.
Probably one of the linens by this artist exhibited by Bakers at the 1903 Arts and Crafts Exhibition (197A, 287, 309). The original design is in the Baker Collection. Block B772, printed with nine blocks.

Baker Record Sample P70/2

116 PANSY, block-printed linen, 1903
Designed by Cecil Millar
32¾ × 33½ (84 × 86) REPEAT: 12½ × 6 (32 × 15.5)

Alternating rows of stylised blue pansies and red tulips with beige leaves and white outlines on a green ground.
Original design is in the Baker Collection. Block B876, printed with five blocks.

Baker Record Sample P84/6 (illus. p.85)

117 PEVENSEY, block-printed linen, 1903
Designed by L.P. Butterfield
15½ × 34 (87 × 37) REPEAT: 11¾ × 6 (30 × 15.5)

Stylised tulip heads in rows within an ogee repeating framework. In shades of green, brown, red and gold with dark red outlines on a natural linen ground.
The blocks were cut for this design in "June 1903". Original design in the Baker Collection. Block B968, printed with four blocks.

Baker Record Sample P126/3

118 ARLESFORD, block-printed linen, 1903
Designed by L.P. Butterfield
47½ × 31 (120 × 78) REPEAT: 14¾ × 29¼ (38 × 75)

Ogee compartments containing stylised flower heads in shades of blue, yellow and pale green, outlined in blue on a white ground.
Designed also to be used as the field design for a tablecloth. There are two designs, signed by Butterfield in the Baker Collection (one for a border). Block B878, twelve blocks were used to print "border, corner and filling".

Baker Record Sample P88/4 (illus. p.90)

119 PETWORTH, block-printed linen, 1903
Designed by L.P. Butterfield
16½ × 31½ (42 × 78) REPEAT: 12 × 12 (31 × 31)

Meandering design of tulip heads and leaves in shades of green, peach, tan, cream and black with black outlines on a red ground.
The original design, which is in the Baker Collection, shows the pattern in a toning colour scheme of blues and greens. Blocks cut "June 1903". A further ground block was cut in 1915 showing the design's continuing popularity. Block B957, printed with seven blocks.

Baker Record Sample P122/4

120 MICKLEHAM, block-printed linen, 1903
Designed by Harry Napper
29 × 31½ (73½ × 80.5) REPEAT: 14¾ × 7½ (38 × 19.5)

Vertical stems are cut diagonally by groups of stylised flowerheads in shades of green, beige and dark red on a white ground.
Original design in the Baker Collection. This pattern shows strongly the influence of Scottish designers. Block B971, printed with four blocks.

Baker Record Sample P118/3

121 GRENADA, block-printed linen, 1903
Designer unknown
51 × 31 (130 × 80) REPEAT: 14½ × 7½ (37 × 19.5)

Stylised cross-sections of capsicum on a ground of sprouting leaves. In mauve and shades of yellow and green on a white ground.
A rare Baker example of the use of an unusual motif, a fashion much pursued by contemporary manufacturers. The original design is in the Baker Collection. Block B964, printed with four blocks.

Baker Record Sample P115/2

122 TIGER LILY, design for a printed textile, watercolour on paper, 1896
Designed by L.P. Butterfield
23 × 16½ (58.5 × 42)

Continuous vertical stems blossoming at intervals with tiger lily flowers. In orange and peach and shades of green and pale blue on a blue ground.
There is an identical design to this in the V&A (E.68-1961).

Baker Collection

124 125

126

122a TIGER LILY, block-printed linen, 1896
Designed by L.P. Butterfield
34 × 32 (87 × 82) REPEAT: 15$\frac{1}{4}$ × 19$\frac{1}{2}$ (39 × 50)

Design as above in shades of pink and green with a green outline on a white ground. Block B427, printed with five blocks.

Baker Record Sample P161/3 (illus. p.92)

123 BAYHAM, block-printed linen, 1903
Designed by L.P. Butterfield
16 × 32 (41 × 82) REPEAT: 14$\frac{1}{2}$ × 14$\frac{3}{4}$ (37 × 38)

Design of pairs of hanging bell-shaped flowers with intersecting stems and leaves. In shades of green with bright pink and purple outlines on a natural linen ground.

The brightness of the red in this design was probably achieved with the use of mordanted dyestuffs. The original design, in which the flowers are in yellow, is in the Baker Collection. Block C39, printed with four blocks.

Baker Record Sample P163/3

124 IPSWICH, block-printed linen, 1903
Designed by W. Warner
25 × 32$\frac{1}{2}$ (63.5 × 82.5) REPEAT: 15 × 14$\frac{1}{2}$ (38 × 37)

An ogival and lozenge pattern showing tulips primulas and other flowers in shades of green, pink, blue, mauve, brown and yellow on a white ground.

The original design is in the Baker Collection. Block B979, printed with seven blocks.
Exhib: V&E.D.A. 1952, Y12 (cat. p.137)

V&A T.60-1953 Given by G.P. & J. Baker Ltd.

125 FRITILLARY, block-printed linen, 1903
Designed by Harry Napper
53 × 31$\frac{1}{2}$ (136 × 80.5) REPEAT: 14$\frac{1}{2}$ × 10 (37 × 26)

Repeating design of groups of three fritillary flowers in shades of green with dark orange.

Block C42, printed with two blocks.

Baker Record Sample P167/5

126 PICOTEE, block-printed linen, 1903
Designed by G.C. Haité
14 × 31 (35.5 × 79) REPEAT: 14$\frac{1}{2}$ × 15$\frac{1}{2}$ (37 × 39.5)

Repeating design of dianthus plants in peach, tan and two shades of green on a cream ground.

Original design in the Baker Collection. Block B975, printed with four blocks.

Baker Record Sample P133/2

ABOVE 135 MARGATE SANDS, *watercolour design for nursery cushions, Houghton 1903.*
LEFT EFFINGHAM, *copper-roller printed cotton c.1898.*
RIGHT 143 WATERLILIES, *watercolour design for printed linen, Harry Napper 1905.*

127 VETCH, block-printed linen, 1904
Designed by G.C. Haité
$15\frac{1}{4} \times 31\frac{1}{2}$ (39 × 81) REPEAT: $14\frac{1}{2} \times 14\frac{1}{2}$ (37 × 37)

Vertical stems with flowers, leaves and intersecting tendrils in dark blue with mint green flowers on a natural linen ground, Block C134, two blocks.

Baker Record Sample P189/4

128 MARGUERITE, block-printed linen, 1903
Designed by G.C. Haité
$15\frac{1}{2} \times 30\frac{1}{2}$ (39 × 79) REPEAT: $14\frac{1}{2} \times 14$ (37 × 36)

Dispersed design of flat-headed marguerite flowers on vertical stems, in shades of green and orange.
Original design, with yellow flowers, is in the Baker Collection. Block B972, five blocks.

Baker Record Sample P123/1

129 ROSE AND CROCUS, block-printed linen, 1903
Designer unknown
$16 \times 31\frac{1}{2}$ (41 × 80) REPEAT: $14\frac{1}{2} \times 7\frac{1}{2}$ (37 × 19.5)

Compartmentalised design showing horizontal rows of tulip-like crocus and roses in shades of green and blue with dark blue outlines on a white ground.
Block C18, printed with six blocks.

Baker Record Sample P145/3

130 Block-printed linen, c.1900
Designed by G.C. Haité
61 × 31 (155 × 79) REPEAT: $14\frac{1}{2} \times 10$ (37 × 26)

Two species of alpine rock plants are repeated in alternating rows providing a strong vertical movement in shades of blue on white.
There are two variations of the design in the Baker Collection, one is signed by the designer. The shaded quality of this design imitates the stencil printed wallpapers very popular at this period. Block B880, printed with two blocks.

Baker Record Sample P85/2 (illus. p.84)

131 GERANIUM, design for a printed textile, watercolour on paper, 1902
Designed by Burnet
$17\frac{1}{3} \times 24\frac{1}{2}$ (44.5 × 63)

A design of trailing ivy and geranium flowers and leaves realistically coloured in pink, red, yellow and green on a white ground.
Inscribed with the name of the design and details of blocks. The designer, otherwise unknown, provided one other design for Bakers for a table cover.

Baker Collection

131a GERANIUM, block-printed linen, 1902
Designed by Burnet
25 × 36 (63.5 × 89) REPEAT: $14\frac{1}{2} \times 36$ (37 × 89)

Design as above in shades of green, pink, red and yellow. Block B851, printed with five blocks.

Baker Record Sample P80/3 (illus. p.93)

132 Design for a printed textile, watercolour and body colour on paper, c.1898
Probably designed by L.P. Butterfield
$17\frac{1}{2} \times 20\frac{3}{4}$ (45 × 53)

All-over design of leaves in shades of dark red, turquoise and lime with dark blue outlines on a blue ground.
Printed at the Swaisland Works exclusively for Liberty & Co. (not, in the case of others included in the catalogue, for Bakers and then sold to Liberty). Block B568, printed with five blocks.

Baker Collection

133 STRAWBERRY, block-printed linen, 1903
Designer unknown
17 × 31 (43 × 79) REPEAT: $14\frac{1}{2} \times 8$ (37 × 20.5)

Wild strawberry plants in stylised arched motifs. In pink, red and shades of green on a white ground.
Used also with a border as a table cover. Blocks cut May 1903. Original design in Baker Collection. Block B951, printed with three blocks.

Baker Record Sample P125/2

134 PEAR, block-printed linen, 1905
Designer unknown
$17\frac{1}{2} \times 31\frac{1}{4}$ (45 × 80) REPEAT: $14\frac{1}{4} \times 7\frac{3}{4}$ (36.5 × 20)

Design of pears hanging from blossomed branches in shades of blue, green, black and white with black outlines on a lilac ground.
The original design is in the Baker Collection. Block C157, cut in "Sept. 1905", fabric printed with five blocks.

Baker Record Sample P231/8

135 MARGATE SANDS, design for printed cushion covers, watercolour and body colour on paper, 1903
Designed by Houghton. Sold through Liberty & Co.
19 × 21 (48 × 53)

A young girl and boy paddle in shallow waters, nurse and mother look on with bathing machines to the right. In orange, blue, white, peach, green, grey, gold with white cliffs in the foreground and bright blue sea and sky.

Printed on "Nursery cushions" for Liberty & Co. a number of which (some designs can be found in Baker print books) were illustrated in Liberty catalogues for the period 1900–1905. This style of figurative borders or friezes became popular at the end of the 19th century for nursery wallpapers. Block B928, printed with fifteen blocks.

Baker Collection (*illus. p.96*)

136 SEE-SAW, design for printed cushion covers, watercolour on paper, 1903
Possibly designed by William Kidd. Sold through Liberty & Co.
$23\frac{3}{4} \times 23\frac{3}{4}$ (60.3 × 60.5)

A Dutch girl and boy play on a see-saw, the roofs of houses can be seen in the background. In shades of brown, dark pink, blue, green, orange, mauve and cream.

The Furnisher magazine for October 1900 illustrates examples of nursery friezes designed by William Kidd. These are very similar to a number of Bakers' designs for nursery cushions, including this example. Block B927, printed with twenty-eight blocks.

Baker Collection

137 PATTERN BOOK OF COPPER ROLLER-PRINTED TEXTILES
Showing Bakers' range from c.1903 to 1914
$17\frac{1}{2} \times 11\frac{1}{2}$ (44.5 × 29.5) Samples approx. $4\frac{1}{4} \times 8$ (11.5 × 20.5)

Bakers' first engraved roller sample book, examples shown are "Chestnut" (see cat. 138 for original design) "Abinger" and "Storrington". The range of designs is the same as those used contemporaneously for block-printing although the scope for larger sized patterns improved with this technique and production was more economic. Examples shown surface nos. 313–315.

Baker Collection

138 CHESTNUT, design for a printed textile, body colour and watercolour on paper, c.1900
Designer unknown
$18\frac{1}{2} \times 15\frac{1}{4}$ (46.5 × 38.5)

Design of sweet chestnut flowers and leaves in shades of green, white, rust and green on an ultramarine blue ground.

Printed by copper roller (313), a small sample of this design as textile can be seen in cat. 137, colours marked in pattern book "yellow, red, pale green, dark green, blotch".

Baker Collection

136

139 EFFINGHAM, copper roller-printed cotton, c.1898
Designer unknown. Printed for Liberty & Co.
$29\frac{1}{2} \times 31\frac{3}{4}$ (75 × 80.5) REPEAT: $15\frac{3}{4} \times 15$ (40 × 38)

Meandering trails of cornflowers and sweet peas in shades of brown, yellow and blue on a white ground.

These colours are variations on those named in the roller pattern book, which include purple and green. Original design in Baker Collection. Roller no. 202. Exhib: Liberty's 1975, D30 (cat. p.48) (*illus. p.96*)

V&A. Circ. 108-1966 Given by Manchester School of Art

140 THE MULGRAVE or BEAUCAIRE, copper roller-printed cotton, c.1905
Designer unknown. Sold through Liberty & Co.
$11\frac{1}{4} \times 7\frac{1}{2}$ (29 × 19) REPEAT: not available

Daffodils, pansies and other flowers in festoons on a white and pink latticed ground. In purple, blue, pinks and greens.

This fabric appears in the Baker roller book named "Beaucaire" (Roller no. 685). This sample, which is of the type supplied by the shop to clients, gives specification of fabric width, pattern number and price.

V&A T.332-1976 Given by Liberty & Co.

141 HYDRANGEA, copper roller-printed cotton, c.1896
Designed by L.P. Butterfield. Printed for Liberty & Co.
$11\frac{1}{4} \times 7\frac{1}{2}$ (29 × 19) REPEAT: not available

Design of realistically drawn hydrangea flowers and leaves in shades of blue and white.

LEFT 154 *Block-printed linen, design bought from Vienna in 1908.*
ABOVE 147 MAY CLUSTER, *block-printed linen, Burn 1907.*

Original design in Baker Collection. This textile appears in Bakers' roller pattern book (no. 71) where the colours are described as "yellow, pink, red, olive and blotch". This sample issued by Liberty & Co. has a label specifying their pattern number, width and price per yard.
Lit: Liberty & Co. catalogue *Cretonnes* c.1906 p.15
Liberty & Co. catalogue c.1910 p.5.
Stuttgart 1980, no. 34, illus p.62 (refers to a sample in Stuttgart Museum GT.6522a).

V&A T.327-1976 Given by Liberty & Co.

142 MERLIN, block-printed linen, 1905
Probably designed by L.P. Butterfield
$16\frac{1}{2} \times 30\frac{3}{4}$ (42 × 79) REPEAT: $9\frac{3}{4} \times 5\frac{1}{2}$ (25 × 14)

Repeating design of stylised, elongated holly leaves with berries in shades of green, blue and orange with blue and white outlines on a green ground.

Block book dates blocks "June 1905". Original design in Baker Collection. Block C151, printed with five blocks.

Baker Record Sample P206/4

143 WATERLILIES, design for a printed textile, watercolour and body colour on paper, 1905
Designed by Harry Napper
$18\frac{1}{4} \times 15$ (46.5 × 38)

Stylised waterlily flowers and leaves arranged in horizontal rows on a figured ground. In shades of yellow, green and beige with a striped ground of pale and mid blue.

Printed with a shaded "rainbow" effect, two new blocks for different grounds were cut in 1906.

Baker Collection (*illus. p.97*)

144

143a WATERLILIES, block-printed linen, 1905
Designed by Harry Napper
18 × 31 (46 × 79) REPEAT: $14\frac{3}{4} \times 10\frac{1}{2}$ (37.5 × 26.5)

Design as above. This sample which is faded in parts shows shaded flowers in lemon fading to white and leaves in green. Background in brown and beige with dark green outlines. Block C182.
Exhib: Cotton Board 1955, 264 (cat. p.49); English Chintz 1960, 453 (cat. p.67)
Lit: *Studio Year Book*, 1911 p.127

V&A T.55-1953 Given by G.P. & J. Baker Ltd.

144 SANDOWN, block-printed cotton, 1903–04
Designed by G.C. Haité
$37\frac{1}{2} \times 30\frac{3}{4}$ (96 × 79) REPEAT: $10 \times 9\frac{1}{2}$ (25.5 × 24.5)

Pattern of diamond-shaped compartments of stylised floral forms in navy blue, pink and shades of green on a white ground. Block C135, printed with three blocks.

Baker Record Sample P211/1

145 RYDE, block-printed cotton, 1905
Designer unknown
$25 \times 31\frac{1}{4}$ (64 × 80) REPEAT: $14\frac{1}{2} \times 7$ (37 × 17.5)

Small, dense all-over design of stylised flowers, in dark blue and shades of green on a white ground.

Block C129, printed with two blocks. This design was adapted for copper roller printing and called "Nutfield" (Roller 683). Original design in Baker Collection.

Baker Record Sample P210/3

146 STRAWBERRY AND GRAPE, block-printed linen, 1906
Designed by Edgar L. Patterson
$14\frac{3}{4} \times 30\frac{1}{2}$ (38 × 78.5) REPEAT: $7\frac{1}{2} \times 4\frac{3}{4}$ (19.5 × 12.5)

Small, dense compartmentalised design of grapes and strawberries in shades of green, blue, pink and black on a white ground.

Original design in the Baker Collection. This artist who also designed wallpapers, woven textiles, furniture and other items for the home sold a number of designs to Bakers, some of which are illustrated in the *Studio Year Book* (1907, 1909). Block C215.

Baker Record Sample P258/4

151

147 MAY CLUSTER, block-printed linen, 1907
Designed by Burn
16 × 31½ (41.5 × 81) REPEAT: 7 × 7½ (18 × 19)

Berries and hawthorn blossom arranged in groups on a wooden trellis, the design has a green and white figured ground. In shades of green, mauve and purple.
Block C235, printed with six blocks.

Baker Record Sample P253/1 *(illus. p.101)*

148 TREFOIL, block-printed linen, 1902–03
Designed by G.C. Haité
21¾ × 34¾ (56 × 89) REPEAT: 10½ × 8 (27 × 21)

Small, dense design of groups of tulip-shaped trees on a leafy ground. In pink on white.
Original design in Baker Collection. Block B901, printed with one block.

Baker Record Sample P105/1

149 Block-printed linen, 1904
Designer unknown
37 × 31¼ (95 × 80) REPEAT: 8½ × 5 (22 × 13)

Dispersed design of repeating, stylised, tree forms in green and blue on a natural linen ground.
Block C174, printed with two blocks.

Baker Record Sample P225/1

150 SQUARE ROSE, block-printed linen, 1904
Designed by Rigby
14¾ × 30 (38 × 78) REPEAT: 14½ × 15¼ (37 × 39)

Repeating design of isolated motifs of stylised roses and leaves in shades of green and blue on a natural linen ground.
Block C26, printed with two blocks.

Baker Record Sample P146/7

151 JEWEL TREE, block-printed linen, 1904
Designer unknown
32¾ × 32½ (84 × 83) REPEAT: 15 × 15 (38.5 × 38.5)

Stylised tree design with borders of floral motifs, in blue, green and dark pink on a cream ground.
Block C44, printed with three blocks.

Baker Record Sample P147/2

152 SALTASH, block-printed linen, 1904
Designer unknown
33 × 31¼ (85 × 80) REPEAT: 6¼ × 7 (16 × 18.5)

Vertically striped design with blocks of decoration of stylised floral motifs in shades of blue and green on a natural linen ground.
Original design in Baker Collection. Block C136, printed with three colours.

Baker Record Sample P200/2

153 Block-printed linen, c.1907
Designer unknown
14¾ × 25¾ (38 × 66) REPEAT: 1½ × 1⅞ (4 × 5)

Repeating design of circular motifs of stylised sprig. White, brown and pink on a green ground.
One of a series of Viennese designs bought from “Siebers” in Vienna. Block C245, printed with three blocks.

Baker Record Sample P272/4

154 Block-printed linen, c.1908
Designer unknown
47 × 31 (119 × 78.5) REPEAT: 4 × 4 (10 × 10)

Geometric design of alternate squares of diamond-shaped and chequered effect in two shades of green and red on a white ground.
The most notable of the group of designs bought from “Siebers” in Vienna, at a time when Viennese design (especially that from the Wiener Werkstätte) led the world. Block C270, printed with three blocks.

Baker Record Sample P299/2 *(illus. p.100)*

155 Block-printed linen, c.1908
Designer unknown
31½ × 32 (80 × 81) REPEAT: 4 × 3 (10 × 8)

Geometric and linear design with yellow triangles and dark green lines on a natural linen ground.
Austrian design bought from “Siebers”.
Block C242, printed with two blocks.

Baker Record Sample P260/4

LEFT HOLLYHOCKS, *block-printed cotton c.1899.* RIGHT *Block-printed cotton and linen cloth c.1910.*

156 Block-printed linen, c.1908
Designer unknown
16 × 31 (40.5 × 78.5) REPEAT: 3 × 3¾ (8 × 9.5)

Geometric design of repeating, spotted motifs in abstract form. In shades of blue and green on a natural linen ground.

Austrian design bought from "Siebers" of Vienna.

Baker Record Sample P328/2

157 HOLLYHOCKS, block-printed cotton, c.1899
Designer unknown
52 × 53½ (132 × 136) REPEAT: 35¾ × 35 (91.5 × 90)

Dense naturalistic design of hollyhocks in purple, mauve, pink, red, maroon, white, cream and beige with shades of green.

The background fabric has a slub effect to look like linen. The type of original naturalistic floral design that Bakers started to produce at the end of the 19th century and which, by 1914, had become their stock in trade.

Baker Record Sample P128/1 (illus. p.104)

158 HOPVINE, block-printed linen and cotton fancy cloth, 1902
Designed by Foord
55½ × 51 (141.5 × 130) REPEAT: 36 × 24½ (92 × 63)

Naturalistic design of hops and ivy in purple, mauve, turquoise and shades of green on a natural linen ground.

Block B885, printed with twenty blocks.

Baker Record Sample P107/1

159 Block-printed linen, 1907–08
Designer unknown
54 × 59¾ (138 × 153) REPEAT: 26 × 28⅓ (67 × 72.5)

Floral motifs and baskets of flowers, printed with a splodgy effect on a diapered ground. In shades of blue, green, brown, red and pink on a mauve ground.

Described in the block books as "Louis XIV reproduction". Printed at a period when reproductions of French historic styles were very popular for interior decoration. Block C244, printed by "60 blocks in 4 sets".

Baker Record Sample P290

160 Block-printed cotton and linen fabric, c.1910
Designer unknown
37½ × 27⅓ (96 × 70) REPEAT: L. 14¾ (Width not available)

Woodland scene with folly in shades of green, black, pink, blue and bluish-white.

Modern design incorporating both fashionable aspects of contemporary interior design preferences with Bakers' own love of the countryside and plants.

Baker Record Sample P199/1 (illus. p.105)

161 GARDEN OF TULIPS, block-printed cotton and linen fancy cloth, 1899
Designed by Hunter
47½ × 61 (121 × 155) REPEAT: 28 × 29½ (72 × 76)

Design of tulips and meandering leaves with a dotted subsidiary design.

Original design in Baker Collection. Block B656, printed with ten blocks.

Baker Record Sample P41/1

161

G.P. & J. Baker – 1914 onwards

At the time of the first world war new synthetic dyestuffs were produced that were faster to light and washing than ever before. This fact, together with outside influences, such as Leon Bakst's exuberant costumes and sets for Diaghilev's Russian Ballet, and, no doubt, a strong reaction against war-time austerity, led to the production in England after 1918 of many textiles in brightly coloured, bold and stylised patterns. "Night Hawk" (cat. 170) is a good example of this style with its flat black areas of silhouetted trees and non-realistically coloured "cottage garden" flowers. The lantern and flying bird are typical of the 1920s vogue for oriental design. Many of these types of design were purchased from the Haward Studio, or other freelance designers such as J.S. Wheelwright. Strong colours set against dark backgrounds were especially popular and even Bakers' more traditional designs were printed in colourways which included bright orange and yellow, fuchsia pink and royal blue on a black background.

By the 1920s, Bakers were well known and valued for their traditional English floral furnishings. Illustrations of their work in publications like the *Studio Year Book* invariably show historic designs taken from such sources as "an old Spanish bedspread" or "a coromandel lacquer screen".[1] A large number of these were prepared in their own design studio at the printworks at Crayford while others were purchased from freelance designers. William Turner's far-eastern influenced designs, often with oriental birds and exotic foliage, for example "Phoenix" (cat. 167), are particularly striking. With slight alterations and re-colouring to suit current fashions, many of these have been in constant production for over 60 years (see cat. nos. 234, 237, 240, 247 and 248). "Phoenix" was one of the fabrics shown by Bakers in Paris in 1925. "In the Grand Palais, the fabrics of G.P. & J. Baker showed a wide range of patterns, many based on historical styles, superlative in quality and sound in craftsmanship."[2]

Such textiles were admirably suited to English domestic architecture of the time. From the early 20th century to the late 1920s the "cottage" style often with Tudor influences predominated. In such settings, these printed

Block-printed linens,
ABOVE 162 PEKIN,
Mr Thomas, 1914,
LEFT 165 MANCHU,
C.T. Lindsay, 1917,
RIGHT 167 PHOENIX,
William Turner, 1918.

A comfortable living room with chairs covered in "Toucans" (234) block-printed linen. "Coombe Cottage", Four Oaks, illustrated in the Studio Year Book *1926.*

linens and cottons were ideal for use as curtaining and chair and cushion coverings (see illustration). The following describes one such room, "The room is tight covered with string-coloured carpet, overspread with Persian rugs, and the chairs have covers of chintz displaying a floral pattern . . . the whole air of the room is one of comfort and well-being."[3]

Techniques

Two main printing methods were used to translate the designs into finished textiles. The linens were usually block-printed. This was a skilled operation, for which the printers served a seven-year apprenticeship. Although this was a slow, and therefore expensive, hand process it did not limit the size of repeats or the number of colours that could be used, unlike the copper roller-printing machines. It was not unusual for up to 150 blocks and thirty colours to be used for one Bakers' design. Most importantly, the particular quality of this careful block-printing gave the designs the liveliness and pleasing appearance of a watercolour wash. Sixty-yard "pieces" of cloth were printed on slate-topped tables of the same length. Production was speeded up at Bakers' works by having two printers work simultaneously on the same fabric, one from either side of the table.

The blocks were usually made at the printworks. By the late 1940s few new designs were being cut and the last set of blocks was made in 1951.

Copper roller-printing was used for the designs with smaller repeats and those which required a greater degree of mechanical accuracy. The

Production at the printworks in the 1930s and '40s.
RIGHT *Block-printing. Colour is taken onto the block from a dye pad or "sieve". The woman behind is the "tierer", her job is to keep the sieve evenly covered with dyestuff.*
BELOW *(left) Twelve-colour machine for copper roller-printing. (right) Hand engraving a copper roller.*

Block-printed linens,
LEFT 169 AZALEAS, *Candioz, 1918,*
BELOW 170 NIGHT HAWK, *the Haward Studio, 1919.*
RIGHT 172 *copper roller-printed linen, 1920.*

maximum number of colours which could be run on one machine was fourteen; several thousand yards of each design had to be printed for the setting up and running of the machines to be economical.

Methods of production at the printworks were extended in the early 1920s by the introduction of surface (wooden-roller) printing, stencil-printing and weaving.

Wooden roller-printing is a mechanised form of block-printing which although in use since the early 19th century, had never replaced high-quality hand block-printing. When printed from a curved surface the dye tends to get squashed out and the end result lacks crisp definition. It was, however, about one third cheaper than block-printing and could operate on a quarter of the amount of power required for copper roller-printing. Machines were installed that could print from six to sixteen colours and there were also some which could use both wood and copper rollers.[4] It was an economic method of printing Bakers' range of popular furnishings like "Wild Duck" (cat. 180) and nursery fabric "Zoo" (cat. 182).[5]

Stencilling, a traditional Japanese method of textile decoration, was done by hand. The stencils were usually made from thin sheets of copper and the dyestuff was simply sprayed or brushed across. This method was only suitable for designs made up of detached units that did not require exact joining of repeats, such as "Stencil Jacobethan" (cat. 178) and the "modern" design "Harebell" (cat. 183). As was usual with this method they are printed on coarse fabric using a limited number of colours.

Screen-printing at the printworks in the 1940s. The dyestuff is forced through the screen mesh by the rubber bladed 'squeegee' which is pushed across the screen from one printer to the other.

In 1932 stencilling was superseded by screen-printing. Connected shapes and continuous lines were now possible as the "stencil" was supported on silk gauze stretched across a wooden frame. The dye-stuff was pressed through the screen with a squeegee (see illus), the mesh of the gauze being so fine that it did not show up in the resulting print. This job was considered unskilled and was done by women.

Screen-printing, like stencilling, was quicker and cheaper to set up than both block and machine-printing. In the 1930s it enabled many British firms to try out short runs of high quality experimental designs that would have been uneconomical to produce by other means.

Screen-printing has become the most important method of printing today. By the late 1950s mechanised "flat bed" systems utilising metal screens and meshes were in use in the textile industry. More recently, printing by fully automatic, continuous, horizontal, rotary screen machines, first used in Holland in 1963,[6] has become widespread.

Weaving

The weaving department was set up and run by Brian Baker. Warp-printed cotton furnishing fabrics known as "Shadow Tissues" (cat. 177) were among its main products in the 1920s and '30s and were immensely popular. The warps were printed by the new wooden roller machines. The subsequent weaving with a plain weft yarn softened the edges of the design and gave it a shadowy appearance.

Power looms in the weaving department, about 1930. The two looms in the foreground are weaving shadow prints (see cat. 177).

LEFT 180a WILD DUCK, *wooden roller-printed jute, Stone, 1928.*
RIGHT 185 PERSIMMON, *design, pencil and watercolour on paper, Mr or Mrs W. Gordon Hunton, 1928.*

2 Greens
2 Yellow Greens
1 Dk Red
1 Pale Red
1 Crimson
1 Yellow
1 Blue
1 Black
18" x 15"
PERSIMMON
3631
2328

Plain cotton and linen fabrics were woven for subsequent printing, and also jacquard-woven furnishings and bedspreads. The latter were tabby woven, often with multicolour random stripes to use up spare yarns. Martin Baker recalls that when he joined the firm in 1948 there were approximately forty plain looms, four dobby looms and about four to eight jacquard looms, and that about fifty people, maybe a fifth of the workforce worked in this department. It is worth noting that all steps in the manufacture from cloth production to finishing could be carried out at Bakers' works.

Design in the last sixty years

By the late 1920s the demand for hectic and brilliant coloured textiles had died away. Subdued and subtle tones led the way into the next decade. The soft colouring and fluid drawing of Hunton's "Feathers" (cat. 186) and "Persimmon" (cat. 185) are a marked contrast to the static flat masses of colour in the Haward Studio's designs of ten years before.

Avant-garde textile designers in Britain were influenced by art and design movements from the Continent, particularly by the streamlined "functional" interiors of modern architects. Severe, sparsely coloured, abstract and geometric designs resulted. Although Bakers did not embrace the extremes of this style, they did bring out an experimental range of purely geometric patterns. "Pillar" (cat. 196) designed by the Silver Studio, and other simple "modern" designs were the first to be printed by screen at Crayford. At the same time a series of elegant glazed cottons were block-printed with figurative forms in muted colourings, sometimes on a dark background. The number of colours used did not exceed six, a serious consideration at a time when the cost of block-printing was becoming prohibitive even for Bakers' exclusive work. These refined designs appealed to the fashionable eclectic interior designers of the day. Hayes Marshall, the writer on interior decoration, used "Laurel Leaf" (cat. 200) in his own study together with the most modern furniture and an abstract hand-knotted rug (illus). Some of the designs for these cottons were the work of internationally known young designers, like "Quills" (cat. 198) by Mea Angerer. The dramatic "Large Lily" (cat. 201) was one of several produced especially for the sophisticated American market.

Already in the 1930s Bakers could boast of a wide market and a high class clientele at home and abroad. Sales were made direct to interior designers and wholesalers. Mr Bloch their agent travelled the length and breadth of Europe carrying large hampers of Baker samples,[7] and in the USA longstanding contacts had been made with important wholesale distributors including Arthur H. Lee Inc., and Bailey & Griffin Inc., and many others in New York.

Towards the end of the '30s there was a marked return to a preference for natural forms in textile design. People were bored with geometric designs, "Geometric patterns are less popular than they were for a year or two, because people have discovered that they are not restful. Designs (including floral ones) that are positive in a delicate, subtle fashion rather than merely emphatic, are coming back – and most of us, I think, are glad. We are a little tired of the black square or circle on a white ground."[8]

They craved for richer and more graceful fabrics to adorn their large window spaces, bare walls and stark furniture. Frank Ormrod's designs met these needs perfectly. "Tropical Fish" (cat. 205) was one of many fish designs which caught the public's imagination. The revolt against "the old modernity" was applauded as a healthy sign. "Together with it goes a much freer use of lovely textiles than has been the case for a very long time . . . there is a new elegance of feeling in the air, a liking for a pardonable effect of richness and luxury and an understanding of the good results which can be got by an alliance of the old and new when creating a liveable modern interior . . .".[9] This wave of nostalgia paved the way for Bakers' decision to concentrate on producing designs based on its collection of historic material.

During the Second World War the production of high-class furnishings was hindered by shortage of labour, lack of raw materials, especially linen, and government restrictions. "Blue and white" (cat. 207) is a rayon, screen-printed during the war for the Utility range. The 1940s in general saw little new textile design.

After the war was over, George Percival Baker "retired" and his nephew Ronald Baker took over both the London office and the task of buying new designs and archive material. Concentrating on using the archive as a design source, he worked closely with Philip Reed and Ernest Skinner, the designers at the printworks. Close contacts with older freelance designers were maintained and new ones formed with the younger generation. A limited number of new designs were still acquired for production. The "contemporary" abstract designs of the 1950s *avant garde* were avoided but elements of their influence were reflected in the layout of designs like "Pastorale" (cat. 214) by Pollet, where rural scenes are placed in irregular shaped "windows". This was a popular design and was copper roller-printed in large quantities on both linen and cotton. In 1952 three of Bakers' "traditional" designs, a broken stripe, "Cherry Stripe" (cat. 235), and "Ferns" (cat. 224), were shown in a leading British textile export magazine with the following caption which sums up well the philosophy on which Bakers' reputation stands today:

> "A sense of style characterises this charming range of printed chintzes from G.P. & J. Baker Ltd. They are an excellent example of the use of an imaginative interpretation of traditional, but not too familiar forms. Coloured exquisitely and printed with great skill, they breathe an air of the past, and yet they have the power to refresh a contemporary interior."[10]

From 1954 onwards, a series of highly acclaimed fabrics, faithfully redrawn from 18th-century plate-printed textiles, were made for F. Schumacher & Co., New York, for the Williamsburg restoration project.

ABOVE 184 CACTUS, *wooden roller-printed glazed cotton, the Haward Studio, 1930.*
LEFT 183 HAREBELL, *stencilled linen, Bruce, 1929.*
RIGHT 186 FEATHERS, *block-printed linen, Mr or Mrs W. Gordon Hunton, 1930.*

The single-colour print cottons "Penn and the Indians", "Bonny Charley" and "Soloman's Seal" (cat. nos. 219–221) are some of the resulting designs.

The bought-in designs of the later 1950s and early '60s include some freely drawn, painterly florals in which the textures of brush and pen marks are carefully reproduced (cat. nos 215–217). They are probably the result of a fashionable movement to use the work of well known fine artists such as Henry Moore and John Piper for repeating textile designs.

In the 1960s Bakers continued to build their reputation for traditional English floral designs and those inspired by historic documents. The archive was the focal point and catalyst of the studio. The choice of colouring was, as always, considered with great awareness of contemporary taste and modern trends. A particularly interesting example was "Open Window" (cat. 52), screen-printed in black and red on white cotton, contrasting with the original of 1810–20 and the copper-roller versions of the 1930s.

Two of Bakers' best known designs date from these years, "Paradise Bird" (cat. 252), a completely revised version of a design made by William Turner from a Chinese wallpaper for Bakers at the beginning of the century, and "Provencal" (cat. 225), a delicate, sensitively drawn pattern from an 18th-century child's bodice. The latter pre-empted the 1970s vogue for smaller scale "country" floral furnishings.

Continuing into the 1970s, patterns from embroideries, woven and printed fabrics were freely borrowed, scales altered and design elements rearranged. "Bosonova" (cat. 227) is a neat transformation of an ancient Peruvian weave (cat. 18) which has resulted in a strikingly modern design. Earlier Baker designs, such as "Pekin" (cat. 162) and 1930s "Feathers" (cat. 229) were redrawn and recoloured. Fragments of a Chinese dragon robe were reassembled with museum advice. The result inspired the dramatic "Emperor's Robe" (cat. 226). Ideas came not only from textiles but from other branches of the decorative arts. The small diaper pattern "Chao" (cat. 231) was found on a Chinese vase and "Thames Bridges" (cat. 228) was drawn from an amalgamation of several old prints.

The 1980s designs displayed and illustrated here (from cat. 238) may be allowed to speak for themselves. Throughout the 20th century there has been a demand for the traditional English floral despite changing tastes in "modern" and "contemporary" decoration. People often found abstract patterns unsympathetic and grew tired of them when they became out of date. Since the 1950s a world-wide preoccupation with restoring and refurnishing historic houses has accelerated a growing interest in and appreciation of the past. Currently the vogue for traditional design has become widespread and Bakers are in the forefront of this revival.

The later history of the firm

After their acquisition by Bakers the Swaislands printworks continued to be partly dependent on printing commissioned by other firms. These have included at different times Brocklehurst-Whiston Amalgamated Ltd., Cresta Silks Ltd., (cat. nos. 193 and 194), Liberty & Co. Ltd., Henry Nathan, Story & Co. Ltd., Tibor Reich, Warner & Sons Ltd., and interior decorators such as Gregory & Co. Ltd., and Mann & Fleming (cat. 204). The work ranged from furnishing and dress fabrics to flags and handkerchiefs, and from short, exclusive hand-blocked lengths to mass-production machine-prints. Bakers' own furnishing fabrics are almost invariably printed on linen or cotton, but for their customers they printed on "a long list of fabrics of other materials, including wool, artificial silk and mohair".[11]

The position of the textile industry in Britain in the 20th century has not been a rosy one. Competition from overseas has been one of the main reasons. The cotton industry in particular, has suffered from increased production of inexpensive mass-produced goods by cheap labour in the developing countries which were once British customers.

Despite a brief boom after the end of the Second World War the situation became worse and in the 1950s many textile manufacturers from spinners to finishers found themselves without sufficient work. In the mid 1950s Story & Co. Ltd., London, went out of business and overnight the Bakers' printworks lost half of its commissioned printing. It was at this time also that the weaving department was found to be uneconomic and was closed. In an attempt to strengthen and consolidate the industry, the government offered financial compensation to firms that went out of business. In 1960 Bakers' board of directors decided to accept the offer and in the spring of the following year the works, with the exception of the engraving shop, were sold to a property developer. Wreckers were brought in to destroy the machinery as the government required proof that equipment had not been sold and could not be used again.

Since the closure of Bakers' own printworks the majority of the linens and cottons have been printed by Stead McAlpin & Co. Ltd. in Carlisle, and Edward Turnbull & Sons Ltd., near Bury, Lancashire.

The engraving shop was retained for a further two years and the copper rollers produced there were sent out for printing. In 1963 there were seven hand engravers ranging in age from twenty-one to fifty-seven. The work done by this department was of the highest quality. The Williamsburg reproduction "toiles" already mentioned are exceptionally fine examples of their last work. These were single-colour prints requiring only two engraved rollers at most. The cost of ten or twelve rollers for a multicoloured print would have been prohibitive for such exclusive designs. On the closing of the department Allan Mingham, head engraver and manager, blamed the demise of copper roller production on a less discerning public and the commercialisation of screen-printing.[12] Screen-printing had been fully automated, and was rapidly becoming the most widely used method of textile printing. Designs photographically transferred to the screens and finer screen meshes meant that almost any pattern could be reproduced.

LEFT 196 PILLAR, *screen-printed linen, the Silver Studio, 1933.*
ABOVE 187 GARDEN AND POOL, *wooden roller-printed linen, 1933.*

The closing of the printworks did not alleviate the financial difficulties as it had been hoped. In January 1964 Bakers were acquired by the textile division of Parker Knoll. This firm had been in business since the 1870s, widely known for its furniture. Douglas Kitching who had been responsible for setting up Parkertex in 1950 and building a strong wholesale business, now became managing director and chairman of G.P. & J. Baker Ltd. (Since his retirement this post has been held by his son, John Kitching.) Bakers' design flair had impressed Douglas Kitching and he was pleased to take advantage of so good an opportunity to expand in the printed textile market.

As design director Ronald Baker remained in London to work in the Studio with Ernest Skinner (who became studio manager), and Ann Lynch who had joined the firm in 1957. Philip Stockford, a widely experienced designer (see cat. 228) joined the studio in 1966. At the end of the following year he became design director after the sudden death of Ronald Baker. As work picked up the studio expanded. When Ernest Skinner retired Ann Lynch succeeded him as studio manager in 1977 directing six full-time young designers, becoming design manager the next year and then design manager and colourist.

After the change of ownership Bakers' London office and warehouse in Giltspur Street was moved to Parker Knoll Textiles headquarters at High Wycombe, Buckinghamshire. The studio was re-established above the Parkertex showroom in Berners Street in London. The new parent company gave Bakers financial backing and the benefit of expert management skills in a closely related field which had led to new openings in export and home markets. Ronald Baker's nephew, Michael Cutcliffe, became an export director[13] while maintaining close links with the studio. Since 1972 the Company has exhibited each year at the Heimtex Exhibition in Frankfurt-am-Main. Bakers now have a solid base from which they are able to concentrate on the development and expansion of their own particular design style.

FRANCIS HINCHCLIFFE

*Bakers' records identify designers by their surnames only; further information is given wherever possible. From cat. 162 onwards only the height of the repeat is given.**

162 PEKIN, block-printed linen, 1914
Designed by Mr Thomas
$54\frac{1}{4} \times 50$ (138 × 127) REPEAT: $73\frac{1}{2}$ (187)*

Swirling dragons and formalised clouds in smoky blues, beiges and black on natural linen. Motifs for this design are taken from 18th and 19th century Chinese imperial dragon robes.

This design was so successful that it was reprinted in the 1940s, '50s and '60s, and redrawn on a reduced scale for screen printing in 1975 (SC776) as the original repeat was too large for screen sizes.

Mr Thomas worked in Bakers' studio at Crayford from about 1896 until 1925. Block C469.

Baker Record Sample P623/3 (illus. p.108)

163 YEDDO, block-printed linen, 1914
Designed by Mr Thomas
$52\frac{3}{4} \times 51\frac{1}{4}$ (134 × 130) REPEAT: $18\frac{1}{2}$ (110)

Mountainous landscape with lake, trees and buildings delicately drawn in the style of a Japanese painting. Subtle shades of grey and brown on natural ground. Block C492.

Baker Record Sample P686/4

164 NORMANDY or APPLEBLOSSOM, block-printed linen, 1915
Designed by C.T. Lindsay
52 × 50 (132 × 127) REPEAT: $18\frac{1}{2}$ (47)

Sprigs of appleblossom, sprays of small pink roses, Red Admiral and Cabbage butterflies on a deep blue background overprinted with a "Japanese" floral pattern in black.

Lindsay designed for textiles and wallpapers, examples of his work are illustrated in the *Studio Year Book of Decorative Arts* 1913 and 1918. His designs show a fresh approach and liberal interpretations from traditional design sources. Block C493.

Baker Record Sample P684/3

165 MANCHU, block-printed linen, 1917
Designed by C.T. Lindsay
52 × 52 (132 × 132) REPEAT: $34\frac{1}{4}$ (87)

An oriental inspired design of vases of flowers, flying parakeets, in brown, blues, red, pink, purple and green with a yellow ochre cross-hatched background on natural linen.

Baker Record Sample P732/4 (illus. p.108)

166 HARBIN, block-printed linen, 1915
Designed by William Turner
$52\frac{3}{4} \times 51\frac{1}{4}$ (134 × 130) REPEAT: $23\frac{3}{4}$ (62.5)

Roundels containing stylised almond blossom, other flowers and butterflies on a diaper patterned background, in blue and black on a natural ground. This design is based on traditional Japanese resist-printed country textiles.

Between 1909 and 1925 Bakers purchased in excess of sixty designs from Turner, most are close adaptations of historic source material. He is best remembered for his imposing large scale designs of birds and foliage, several of which are still in production. He also designed for wallpapers and examples of these as well as his fabric designs are illustrated in the *Studio Year Book of Decorative Arts* 1914–16, 1920, 1925 and 1926. Block C504.

Baker Record Sample P682/3

167 PHOENIX, block-printed linen, 1918
Designed by William Turner
95 × 58 (240 × 147) REPEAT: 59 (150)

Phoenixes and cranes with trees and foliage in shades of buff and brown with small areas of muted yellow, green and orange on natural linen. Taken from E.60-1911 in the V&A, a hanging scroll, watercolour painted on silk, Chinese 16th–17th century (with a 14th-century date).

This impressive large-scale design required 143 blocks to print one repeat. Block C610.

Bakers' 1983 range includes a screen-printed version of Phoenix on glazed cotton (BO341).
Exhib: English Chintz, 1960 (470)
Lit: Paris 1925.

V&A T.377-1934 Given by the British Institute of Industrial Art (illus. p.109)

168 Design, watercolour and gouache on paper, 1918
$19\frac{1}{2} \times 33\frac{3}{4}$ (49 × 86)

Farmyard scene of chickens in realistic colours.

Unfortunately Bakers do not have a sample of this naturalistic nursery fabric which they printed by copper roller (1689), probably on to cotton.

Design 3818, Baker Collection

169 AZALEAS, block-printed linen, 1918
Designed by Candioz
$50 \times 58\frac{1}{4}$ (127 × 148) REPEAT: $24\frac{1}{2}$ (62)

All over design of white, and red striped mauve pink, azalea blooms on brown branches with blue leaves and brightly coloured swallow-tail, fritillary and other butterflies against black.

LEFT *(above)* 210 STAPLER'S PEACOCK, *block-printed linen, Wynborough, 1948.* *(below)* 216 NARCISSUS, *design, ink and gouache on paper, Wilson, 1959.* RIGHT 214 PASTORALE, *copper roller-printed linen, Pollet, 1957.*

This, and the following fabrics show the postwar fashion for strong images and bright colours, often set against a black background. Block C615, printed with twenty-eight blocks.

Baker Record Sample P834/1 (illus. p.112)

170 NIGHT HAWK, block-printed linen, 1919
Designed by the Haward Studio
$43\frac{3}{4} \times 50\frac{1}{2}$ (111 × 128) REPEAT: $38\frac{1}{2}$ (98)

English garden flowers (roses, hollyhocks and hydrangeas) in strong pinks, mauves and blues, with green and black silhouette foliage, lantern, and bird in mid flight.

The Haward Studio was established in 1892 in Chiswick by Sidney Haward, formerly chief assistant to Arthur Silver, was carried on by Eric and James Haward and is currently run by Anne Haward. They designed wallpapers and textiles with a leaning to traditional English florals, although the changing demands of fashion proved them a versatile firm. Bakers were a frequent customer until the early 1930s. Block C621 printed with fifty-nine blocks.

Baker Record Sample P853/2 (illus. p.113)

171 BLACK HOODED CROW, block-printed linen, 1920
Designed by the Haward Studio
$53\frac{1}{2} \times 50\frac{1}{2}$ (136 × 128) REPEAT: 31 (79)

Hooded crows sitting in the branches of an exotic flowering tree. Greys, white, mauves, pinks, bright blues and touches of bright orange, yellow and turquoise on a natural ground. Block C649, printed with fifty-seven blocks.

Baker Record Sample P872/2

172 Copper roller-printed linen, 1920
$54 \times 48\frac{3}{4}$ (137 × 124) REPEAT: 19 (48.5)

Oriental blossoming tree in vase with mirror and lantern. Green, turquoise, yellow, orange, black, greys, brown and bright fuchsia pink.

Lanterns were popular motifs at this time and frequently appear on textiles. Copper roller 1777.

Baker Record Sample P932/5 (illus. p.113)

173 THE POOL, block-printed linen, 1920
Designed by J.S. Wheelwright
$53 \times 51\frac{1}{4}$ (135 × 130) REPEAT: $23\frac{1}{2}$ (60)

Terns and dippers at the edge of a pool amongst lush foliage. The predominant colours are pink and blue, the background is black.

This design, redrawn by Claire Wooldridge for screen-printing in 1977, is in current production (A0909 and R1170) now called "The Dippers".

174

176

Wheelwright was a freelance textile designer working from Tonbridge in Kent from about 1910. He enjoyed a reputation for versatility and excellence in design and colour. In the 1930s he patented machinery for silk screen-printing. Block C653, printed with thirty-five blocks.

Baker Record Sample P880/7

174 PERSIAN GARDEN, block-printed linen, 1923
Designed by J.S. Wheelwright
$45\frac{3}{4} \times 52\frac{1}{2}$ (116 × 133) REPEAT: $43\frac{1}{4}$ (110)

Rocky landscape with trees, inspired by Persian designs. Blue green, bright apple green, browns, brownish pink, beiges and blue grey with black outlines and dark green background. Block C702, printed with twenty blocks.

Baker Record Sample P984/4

175 CHEVRON STRIPE, block-printed linen, 1922
$66\frac{1}{2} \times 25\frac{1}{2}$ (169 × 64.5) not full width REPEAT: 13 (33.5)

Angled bands of alternating colours with motifs from an oriental carpet. This trial piece shows two colourways, blue and green above and pinky red, blue and green below, on a coarse woven natural linen. Block C680.

Baker Record Sample P944

176 EGYPTIAN, block-printed linen, 1923
Designed by Kolland
$59\frac{3}{4} \times 32$ (152 × 81) REPEAT: $29\frac{1}{2}$ (75)

Horizontal bands containing a charioteer with bow and arrow and stylised plants, in fawn, browns, black, yellow, blue and pale salmon pink.

Howard Carter and Lord Carnarvon's discovery of the tomb of Tutankhamen in 1922 sparked off a new craze for ancient Egyptian style decoration for everything from architecture to dress. Bakers were quick off the mark with this furnishing design. Block C703, printed with seventeen blocks.

Baker Record Sample P964/4

177 Shadow print cotton, 1925
51 × 32 (130 × 81) REPEAT: $27\frac{1}{2}$ (70)

Exotic flowering branches and jungle birds in greens, browns, red and blue.

The shadow effect is achieved by printing, in this case by surface roller, the warp threads of the fabric prior to weaving. Both processes were carried out at Bakers' printworks.

Bakers exhibited three warp-printed cottons, price 4s 6d per yard, at the British Institute of Industrial Art Autumn Exhibition Illustrating British Industrial Art for the Slender Purse (143–5) at the V&A in 1929. The goods shown in this exhibition were not necessarily cheap, but ones which provided good quality for money. Surface S50.

Baker Record Sample S121/2

178 STENCIL JACOBEAN, stencilled linen, 1924
$53 \times 50\frac{1}{2}$ (135 × 128) REPEAT: $46\frac{1}{2}$ (118)

Design of meandering stems with large curling leaves adapted from a late 17th-century English crewelwork embroidered bedhanging. The different embroidery "filling" stitches are represented by dots, shading and zig-zag lines. Two shades of blue, with loose fitting yellow blotch, on natural coarse linen.

In the late 19th and the first half of the 20th century "Jacobethan" designs were popular and produced in large numbers. This "Olde Englishe" style was much decried by exponents of the modern movement. Stencil S30.

Baker Record Sample P983/4

179 ANIMALS, block-printed jute, 1928
$51\frac{1}{2} \times 50$ (131 × 127) REPEAT: $51\frac{1}{2}$ (131)

Curious animals, insects and plants in browns, deep pinks, green, blue and sludgy yellows with green trail on natural coarse linen.

This is an enlarged adaptation from an English early 17th-century embroidered long cover (V&A T.53-1926).

Redrawn by Barbara Edelman about 1980 for screen-printing and renamed "Nonsuch" after Nonsuch Palace, an Elizabethan house now demolished. Block C824.

Baker Record Sample R271/1

180 FLYING DUCK, design for a printed textile, gouache on paper, 1927 or 28
Designed by Stone
$35\frac{1}{2} \times 30$ (90.5 × 76)

Pair of mallard ducks in flight against silhouetted trees and pagoda. Purple trees outlined in dark blue with pinkish grey sky. Eleven colours are coded on the bottom edge.

Purchased from Stone in January 1928 for fifteen guineas.

Design 1829, Baker Collection

LEFT *curtains and seat covers made from* EMPEROR'S ROBE (226) *screen-printed linen, Ernest Skinner, 1973.*
ABOVE 225 PROVENCAL, *copper roller-printed cotton, Ernest Skinner, 1968.*
RIGHT 252 PARADISE BIRD, *copper roller-printed linen, Ann Lynch, 1960.*

180a WILD DUCK, wooden roller-printed jute, 1928
Designed by Stone
52 × $31\frac{3}{4}$ (132 × 81) REPEAT: $29\frac{1}{2}$ (74.5)

Design as above but with olive green foliage, brown tree trunks outlined with cobalt blue, pale pink pagoda and turquoise sky suggestive of sunset.

Wooden roller-printing was cheaper than hand block-printing and was ideally suited to the production of longer runs of cheaper designs. This design ran until 1931. Wooden roller S109.

Baker Record Sample R269/2 (illus. p.116)

181 SHIPS, wooden roller-printed jute, 1928
52 × 32 (132 × 81) REPEAT: $30\frac{1}{4}$ (77)

Tropical island scene with palm trees and full rigged sailing ships. Browns, turquoise greens, blue and pale purple.

This is probably the French design "Bateaux" which was purchased in December 1926 from Seguy. Surface S102.

Baker Record Sample R175/3

182 JARDIN ZOO or ZOO, design, watercolour and ink on paper, 1929
Designed by Philip J.T. Reed
$33\frac{1}{4}$ × $31\frac{1}{2}$ (84.5 × 80)

Nursery design with camels, elephants and other zoo animals, balloon and ice-cream seller and children, in naturalistic colours. Sixteen colours are listed.

Wooden roller-printed (S124) on cotton (A23), 1930–33. The height of the design has been reduced by removing thin horizontal strips at regular intervals. This allowed for the discrepancy in repeat height between the application of the design to the wooden rollers and the finished roller built up with metal strips and felt ready for printing. Designs were usually drawn taking this slight adjustment into account.

Later on until his retirement in about 1962–63 Mr Reed was in charge of Bakers' Studio at Crayford. He worked as a freelance designer and also in the Haward Studio.

Design 2203, Baker Collection

183 HAREBELL, stencilled linen, 1929
Designed by Bruce
54 × 52 (137 × 132) REPEAT: $27\frac{1}{2}$ (70)

Loosely arranged groups of stylised wild flowers and foliage in bright pink, peach, and three shades of blue on natural linen.

An uncomplicated design with medium size flat

181

182

areas of colour necessary for this method of production. Stencil s88.

Baker Record Sample R274/1 (illus. p.120)

184 CACTUS, wooden roller-printed glazed cotton, 1930
Designed by the Haward Studio
$53\frac{1}{2} \times 31$ (136 × 79) REPEAT: $23\frac{3}{4}$ (60)

Beige, brown and aubergine cacti close packed, with green leaves, pink flowers and a very pale grey green blotch.

Cacti were a popular motif, Bakers had "Cactus Bud" by Miss Hunter, "Cactus" by Miss Moller, and this Haward design in production simultaneously. Surface s137.

Baker Record Sample F452/5 (illus. p.120)

185 PERSIMMON, design for a printed textile, pencil and watercolour on paper, 1928
Designed by Mr or Mrs W. Gordon Hunton
$22\frac{1}{2} \times 25\frac{1}{2}$ (57.5 × 6.5)

Branches of persimmon fruits and blossoms in muted bluey greens and orange browns. Twelve different colours are listed.

Purchased in January 1929 for ten guineas. Mr and Mrs W. Gordon Hunton were freelance designers working from their home in Aylesbury, Buckinghamshire. Three of Bakers' cottons and linens by Mrs Hunton were exhibited at the British Industry in Art Exhibition at the Royal Academy, 1935 (2182, 2207 and 2218) together with one of her husband's designs for Turnbull and Stockdale Ltd. (2078). Mr Hunton's work is illustrated in *Studio Year Book* 1919 and 1920, he was also the author of *English Decorative Textiles*, 1930.

Design 3631 Baker Collection (illus. p.117)

185a PERSIMMON, copper roller-printed cotton, 1929 or 1930.
Designed by Mr or Mrs W. Gordon Hunton
$54\frac{1}{2} \times 3\frac{1}{2}$ (138 × 80) REPEAT: 18 (46)

Design and colours as above with addition of beige blotch.

By the late 1920s the brash colours of the previous decade were being cast aside in favour of softer shades and neutral tones.

The high quality of workmanship at Bakers' printworks can be seen by looking at how faithfully this delicately drawn and subtly shaded design has been transferred on to cloth. Copper roller 2328.

Baker Record Sample A221

186 FEATHERS, block-printed linen, 1930
Designed by Mr or Mrs W. Gordon Hunton
$54\frac{1}{4} \times 53$ (138 × 135) REPEAT: 35 (89)

Pale grey ostrich feathers surrounded by loosely drawn overblown roses and other flowers in soft mauves, reds and mustard, with pale blue and fawn leaves on a pale yellow background. Block c847, printed in sixteen colours with thirty-two blocks.

Baker Record Sample R302/1 (illus. p.121)

187 GARDEN AND POOL, wooden roller-printed linen, 1933
Possibly designed by Mr or Mrs W. Gordon Hunton
$25\frac{1}{2} \times 30\frac{1}{2}$ (65 × 78) REPEAT: $25\frac{1}{2}$ (65)

English garden scene with round pool and stone steps, garden flowers including lupins and rock plants in pinks, blues, yellows and white with green foliage and trees, on an undyed ground.

The 1920s saw a widening interest in the new, and particularly English, vogue for informal or "cottage" style gardens, often featuring herbaceous borders and rock gardens. It is not surprising that such a delightfully decorative subject should find its way on to numerous textiles in the late 1920s and early '30s. Surface s210.

Baker Record Sample R746/1 (illus. p.125)

188 Pattern book of copper roller-printed furnishing and dress fabrics, 1924–28
$12\frac{1}{2} \times 9\frac{1}{2}$ (31.5 × 24)

This book was kept at the printworks and includes some printing jobs done for firms other than Bakers themselves. It is shown open at two brightly coloured prints on cotton of 1925–26; 2033 a small repeating pattern of bands of abstract "roses", and 2034 a tree design for furnishing.

Baker copper roller book 187 to 216

189 Copper roller-printed cotton, 1925
$54 \times 32\frac{1}{4}$ (137 × 82) REPEAT: $5\frac{3}{4}$ (14.5)

Repeating pattern of a pair of cherries on a twig, in pink, red dark blue green, grey green and mustard.

This fabric would have been glazed. Copper roller 2269.

Baker Record Sample X702/1

190 CRYSTAL LINING, copper roller-printed cotton, 1929
$53 \times 34\frac{1}{2}$ (135 × 87) REPEAT: $1\frac{1}{2}$ (4)

Small geometric design in black and dark pink on a beige dyed ground.

LEFT 229 FEATHERS, *screen-printed glazed cotton, Ann Lynch, 1976.*
RIGHT 233 BAMBOO AND BLOSSOM, *screen-printed cotton, Ann Lynch, 1977.*

This fabric would have been glazed. Copper roller 2029.

Baker Record Sample X702/1

191 LEAF, copper roller-printed glazed cotton, 1931

$52\frac{3}{4} \times 30\frac{3}{4}$ (134 × 78) REPEAT: $5\frac{3}{4}$ (14.5)

Repeating leaf motif in pale beige with a printed grey blue ground. Copper roller 2424.

Baker Record Sample F558/3

192 FADELESS GARDEN, copper roller-printed cotton, 1931

54 × 32 (137 × 81.5) REPEAT: 7 (18)

Hollyhocks, flags and other cottage garden flowers, with circular stone edged flower bed, in clear, bright pinks, blues, yellow, green and mauve on natural ground.

Probably "Small Garden", a design purchased from Janet Dean in February 1931 for four guineas.

Rapid advances in dye technology led to many claims that colours were fast. These were often reflected in the names given to fabrics by such words as "sunfast" and "fadeless". Copper roller 2409.

Baker Record Sample A18/1

193 Pattern-book of block impressions on paper, 1914–35

$22\frac{1}{2} \times 19\frac{1}{2}$ (57 × 50)

This book contains a variety of designs for furnishing and dress fabrics, handkerchiefs and small flags, printed for Bakers themselves and for print customers such as Gregory and Co. and Brocklehurst Whiston Amalgamated Ltd.

The top two impressions shown, C883 semi-abstract ballerinas in two colours, and C884 "Pitcher" in four colours, were produced for Cresta Silks Ltd, customer number 60 (see cat. 194).

C885 is Bakers' own design, 10 being the code number for their London showroom.

Baker block book C547 to D192

194 CHERRY ORCHARD, PITCHER and PHALANX, three different designs block-printed on silk, 1930–31

Designed by Paul Nash for Cresta Silks Ltd. and printed by G.P. & J. Baker Ltd.

REPEATS: $11\frac{1}{2}$ (29), $3\frac{3}{4}$ (9.5) and $\frac{5}{8}$ (1.5) respectively

Small abstract and semi-abstract repeating patterns in various colourways.

Some of Paul Nash's drawings for these designs are in the V&A's Department of Prints and Drawings (Circ. 348, 316 and 321-1975).

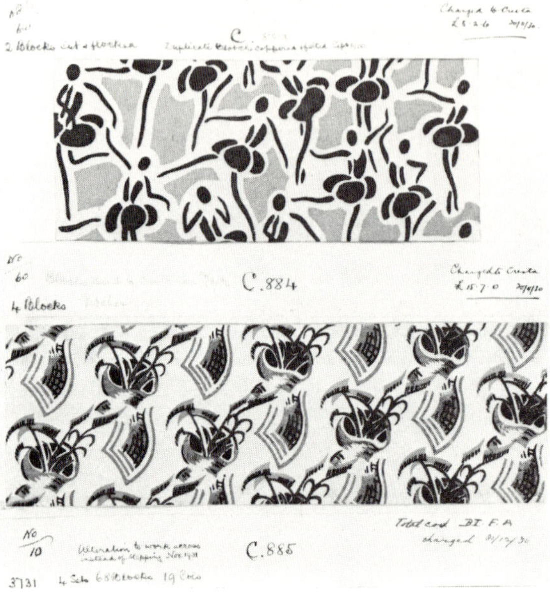

193

198

Cresta Silks Ltd., founded by Tom Heron in 1929, was an innovative firm which engaged well-known *avant-garde* artists, such as Paul Nash, to produce designs for their fabrics. These fabrics were made up into garments at Cresta's own factory in Welwyn Garden City and retailed through their own chain of shops.
Exhib: Nash 1975
Lit: *Dorland Hall*, 1933, p.126
Blocks C856, C884 and C914

V&A Circ. 312 and a-1975. Circ. 464, 466a and 466d-1962. Given by the Paul Nash Trust.

195 WAVERTREE, screen-printed glazed cotton, 1933
36 × 52¾ (91 × 134) REPEAT: 15¾ (40)

One colour print of an abstract pattern of vertical undulating lines with shading. The colour, eau-de-nil on white, is typical of the early 1930s. Bakers began screen-printing in 1932 and this is one of their first examples.

Baker Record Sample F66 4/5

196 PILLAR, screen-printed linen, 1933
Designed by the Silver Studio (see p.83)
54¼ × 53½ (138 × 136) REPEAT: 14½ (37)

Vertical stripes with horizontal curved bands in red, pink and black on natural rough textured "ripple cloth" linen.

In 1934 Bakers printed another Silver Studio geometric design. Both were exhibited at Burlington House in 1935 (1843 & 2076) and described in the catalogue as "modern". They were sold for 6 shillings and 9 pence per yard.

Rex and his brother Harry directed the Silver Studio from 1901. The history of this studio is documented in the Silver Studio exhibition catalogue, 1980. Bakers used many of their designs from the later 1920s onwards.

Baker Record Sample R445/1 (illus. p.124)

197 SPRINGS, wooden roller-printed linen, 1936
53½ × 52½ (136 × 133) REPEAT: 12 (30)

Horizontal bands of spring coils in beige and two shades of brown on natural rough textured "ripple cloth" linen. Surface S358.

Baker Record Sample R482/4

198 QUILLS, block-printed glazed cotton, 1934
Designed by Mea Angerer
54¼ × 52¾ (138 × 134) REPEAT: 19½ (50)

Group of three upright feathers arranged in half drop repeat. Short parallel brush strokes indicate the texture and lightness of the feather. These marks are echoed on the ground. Brown, white, two shades of pink and a pale yellow background.

This design was also produced as a weave (J171).

Miss Angerer was a pupil of Professor Josef Hoffmann at the Kungstgewerbeschule in Vienna. Some of her designs were produced by the Wiener Werkstätte while others were sold in Europe and America. In 1928, at the age of twenty-three she came to England where she worked for eighteen months with Eaton Rural Fabrics Ltd. before continuing as a free-lance designer. Block C998.

Baker Record Sample F560/7

199 LACE, block-printed glazed cotton, 1934
Designed by the Silver Studio
55½ × 52½ (141 × 133) REPEAT: 25 (63)

Floating lace frills, white and pale shades of coffee, against a darker coffee coloured background.
Block D13.

Baker Record Sample F660/6

200 LAUREL LEAF or SILHOUETTE LEAF, block-printed glazed cotton, 1935
Designed by the Silver Studio
53 × 52 (135 × 132) REPEAT: 23½ (59.5)

Trailing leaf design in shades of green and beige on a prune coloured background.

H.G. Marshall of Fortnum and Mason and author or *Interior Decoration Today*, published by F. Lewis Ltd., 1938, used identical fabric in his study. The room had natural canvas covered walls, aubergine· fitted carpet, a hand-knotted modern rug and built-in furniture specially made by Betty Joel Ltd. (see illus. reproduced from *Interior Decoration Today*) Block D82.

Baker Record Sample F735/5

200

LEFT 237a HAN *and* 237 HANKOW *co-ordinating screen-printed linen unions, Claire Wooldridge, 1979.* RIGHT 240 ROCKBIRD, *screen-printed linen union, Bakers' studio, 1981.*

201 LARGE LILY, block-printed glazed cotton, 1935
Manufactured for A.H. Lee
$51\frac{1}{2} \times 25$ (131×63.5) half width REPEAT: $34\frac{1}{2}$ (88)

Huge trumpet-shaped lily flowers and buds in three pale shades of green set against a dark maroon background.

This and cat. 202 are from a group of smart sophisticated designs in fashionable colours printed for the American market. Block D89.

Baker Record Sample F715/4

202 LARGE LEAF, block-printed glazed cotton, 1935
Manufactured for A.H. Lee
40×25 (102×63.5) half width REPEAT: $31\frac{1}{2}$ (80)

Column of hart's-tongue fern leaves in flat areas of colour. Three shades of pale grey, pale cream and palest pink. Block D92.

Baker Record Sample F730/1

203 PILLAR DRAPERY, screen-printed glazed cotton, 1937
Designed by the Silver Studio
$51\frac{1}{2} \times 50\frac{1}{2}$ (131×128) REPEAT: $23\frac{1}{2}$ (60)

Stone coloured Corinthian columns set in a mass of crumpled and draped cloth in shades of blue.

This design has a contemporary surreal quality, however the idea of using crumpled fabric as a textile design was not a new one and dates back to the 1850s. Screen SS106.

Baker Record Sample F910/3

204 Pattern-book of block impressions on paper, late 1930s to early 1950s
19×14 (48×36)

The right-hand open page shows D277, "Salamander", a surreal design of salamanders and trailing vines sprouting human hands with bright red lacquered nails. This was a special contract printing done in 1937 for the interior decorators Mann and Fleming on behalf of Edward James. Only two pieces (approx. 120 yards) were printed. Mr James recalls that he gave the fabric to Salvador Dali for his Paris apartment.

D267 (left-hand page) is a floral with roses and fuchsias.

Baker block book 3, D255 to D606

203

204

205

207

205 TROPICAL FISH, block-printed, 1939
Designed by Frank Ormrod
52 × 32 (132 × 81) REPEAT: 29 (74)

Underwater scene of seaweed and fish in green, brown, pale yellow and pinky red set against a dark maroon background.

Reprinted by screen in 1967 (SC1967). Frank Ormrod was a painter and designer. Block D364.

Baker Record Sample A232/1

206 MAGNOLIA, block-printed glazed cotton, 1939
Designed by Frank Ormrod
52 × 32½ (132 × 83) REPEAT: 26½ (67)

Dense magnolia blossoms and foliage in yellows, browns, beiges, off-white, and pink against a pale reseda green background. Block D371.

Baker Record Sample F978/2

207 BLUE AND WHITE, screen-printed rayon and cotton, 1940
Designed by Williamson
50 × 25 (127 × 64) REPEAT: 13½ (34)

Pale blue laurel leaf swags and bows with superimposed linear floral motif in black.

A green colourway of this design is stamped with the war-time Utility mark.

Bakers have only broken their tradition of printing exclusively on natural fibres for one small range of economic two-colour screen prints in modern figurative designs by Williamson and Davidson. These are on shiny surfaced rayon fabric which had been available throughout the 1930s but was generally considered a cheap alternative. The shortage of linen supplies during the war may have prompted Bakers to use this fabric. Screen SC341.

Baker Record Sample A301/3

208 ARALIA, block-printed linen, 1941
Designed by Josef Frank
118 × 60½ (300 × 154) REPEAT: 28½ (72)

Large, trailing, stylised passion-flower in blue, green, orange and yellow. Selvages inscribed "SVENSK TENN STOCKHOLM" and "KOMP JOSEF FRANK Printed in England".

Josef Frank (1885–1967) was a leading Austrian architect and designer of furniture, glassware, lamps, textiles and wallpapers. He settled in Sweden in 1934 and worked in close collaboration with Svensk Tenn, an exclusive interior design shop. Examples of his work are illustrated in almost every edition of the *Studio Year Book of Decorative Art* since 1924. A commemorative exhibition of his work held at the

Swedish Museum of Fine Arts in Stockholm in 1968, a year after his death, heralded him as a major influence on the development of Swedish interior design.

Ten Frank designs were printed by Bakers from 1939–41. Several had previously been printed about 1930 for Frank's own interior design firm, Haus und Garten, in Vienna (the V&A has samples Circ. 823 to 831-1967). Block D397, Baker pattern R607.

Lent by Svensk Tenn, Stockholm

209 LANDSCAPE, screen-printed cotton, 1941
55 × 51½ (140 × 131) REPEAT: 21¼ (54)

Rural landscape with lane and trees in shades of green and grey.

An insubstantial romantic rendering of a traditional view; a strong reaction against the functionalist designs of the previous decade. Screen SS317.

Baker Record Sample A396/3

210 STAPLER'S PEACOCK, block-printed linen, 1948
Designed by Wynborough
41 × 48 (104 × 122) REPEAT: not available

Peacock, with one wing outstretched and tail half unfolded, perched in a blossoming tree. Blues, greys, white, touches of red and a dusty pink background.

Although different in inspiration this design has the same feeling of restlessness as cat. 209. Block D535.

Baker Record Sample R671 (illus. p.128)

211 Bedspread, machine-woven linen and cotton, about 1946
89 × 103 (226 × 262) including fringes

Weft woven multi-coloured bands. Linen warp fringes are at top and bottom, sides are unstitched selvages.

Bedspreads were manufactured in the weaving department at the printworks before and after the war. Unfortunately all the weaving records, except for one damaged sample book, have been lost.

Lent by Mr C.M. Cutcliffe

211a Jacquard-woven figured damask, linen and cotton, 1950s
16 (irregular) × 50 (41 × 127)

Bunches of grapes, shell pink and cream. J301.

Lent by Mr C.M. Cutcliffe

LEFT 243 SAKARI,
screen-printed cotton,
Wendy Leighton, 1982.

209

213

212 CORN, design for a printed textile, watercolour and gouache on paper, 1950
Manufactured for A. H. Lee
$37\frac{1}{2} \times 50$ (95×127)

Boldly drawn all over design of maize with green leaves and yellow cobs on a white ground. Seven colours are coded on the side. This design was screen-printed on cotton (A451).

Baker Collection

213 TIVOLI, screen-printed glazed cotton, 1955
Designed by Morris
$53 \times 50\frac{1}{2}$ (134×128) REPEAT: 24 (61)

Overgrown garden with classical statues and urns, in beiges, black, grey and pinks. Screen 356SC.

Baker Record Sample B232/7

214 PASTORALE, copper roller-printed linen, 1957
Designed by Pollet
55×51 (140×130) REPEAT: $19\frac{1}{2}$ (50)

Four monochrome (grey and white) rural scenes, including river, boat, houses and trees, within "frames" separated by floral bouquets. Brick red, pale tints of yellow, blue and green.

A 1950s "contemporary" arrangement with traditional imagery. Copper roller 3231.

Baker Record Sample R846/2 (illus. p.129)

215 PEONY AND LABURNUM, screen-printed cotton satin, 1959
Designed by Pollet
$36\frac{1}{4} \times 49\frac{1}{2}$ (92×126) REPEAT: $17\frac{3}{4}$ (45)

Repeat of a loosely painted contemporary floral arrangement in dusky pinks, dark reddish brown and acid yellow with green foliage. The brushmark textured background is in pale pink and grey.

Large showy florals were in vogue in the late 1950s and early 1960s. Screen 559SC.

Baker Record Sample A579/4

216 NARCISSUS, design for a printed textile, ink and gouache on paper, 1959
Designed by Wilson
27×34 (68.5×87)

Slender bunches of narcissi tied and intertwined with ribbon. Ten colours for printing are listed, 1 blotch (black), 1 yellow, 1 red, 2 blues, 1 green, 2 fawns, 1 grey and 1 print.

There is a stamped geometric mark in orange, presumably the designer's mark.

Baker Collection (illus. p.128)

218

220

216a NARCISSUS, copper roller-printed glazed cotton, 1959
Designed by Wilson
$52\frac{1}{2} \times 32$ (133×82) REPEAT: $23\frac{1}{2}$ (60)

Design as above but in white, blue, yellow, black and shades of coffee brown with a pale pea green background. Copper roller 1359m.

Baker Record Sample B297/5

217 SWEET WILLIAM, screen-printed cotton satin, 1963
Designed by Danny Harrison
$35 \times 50\frac{1}{2}$ (89×128) REPEAT: 24 (60.5)

Single flower stems arranged in half drop repeat on olive green with grasses in darker green.

Danny Harrison is a freelance designer of textiles and wallcoverings. After leaving the Royal College of Art in 1952 he sold several floral designs to Ronald Baker. Although new, his work has been strongly influenced by Japanese drawing. An award from the Manchester Cotton Board enabled him to visit Japan for three months. Finding it much to his liking he stayed on and worked there, mainly for American companies, for three years. Screen 261SC.

Baker Record Sample A621/2

218 STAR OF THE ROAD, copper roller-printed cotton, 1952
Drawn by Ernest Skinner or Philip Reed
62 × 31 (158 × 78) REPEAT: 21 (53)

Rural scene with a lady in a horse-drawn carriage in black, greys and brown, set in an oval frame of roses, lily of the valley, pansies and violets in green, white, and violet. The ground is beige scattered with small green rosebuds.

Based on a print published by Nathaniel Currier, New York, 1849. Currier later formed a partnership with James Ives and together they became well known for their vast output of lithographs depicting contemporary American life and history. Interest in their work was revived in the 20th century by Harry T. Peters author of *Currier and Ives* 1942. In the 1940s and '50s Bakers produced several "Currier and Ives" designs, other titles include "Bird Dogs", and "Central Park in Winter". Some were produced like "Star of the Road" in Bakers' studio, while others were commissioned from the Silver Studio. Copper roller 1252m.

Baker Record Sample B161/2

219 PENN AND THE INDIANS, copper roller-printed cotton, 1959
Drawn by Phillip Reed, manufactured for the Williamsburg Restoration Inc.
111 × 34 (282 × 86) REPEAT: 29½ (75)

Monochrome scene depicting William Penn's treaty with the Indians, in dark brown on white. Reproduction of a mid 1780s plate-printed textile, designed after a painting by Benjamin West, engraved by John Hall, published London 1775.

Initially produced through F. Schumacher & Co., New York, as part of a series of reproduction fabrics for the Williamsburg Restoration Inc. They called it "William Penn Toile". In 1953, on receiving "The Aviary", the first in the series, John Upshur, director of merchandising at Colonial Williamsburg wrote to Schumachers praising the high quality of Bakers' work: "The committee was unanimous in expressing the opinion that this was one of the finest reproductions ever presented . . . If the committee ever presented awards, this reproduction would surely merit the golden cross. Everything about it is beautifully executed . . ."

An original piece of textile with this design, from the collection of Colonial Williamsburg, Virginia, USA, was exhibited at the V&A 1960 (177) and is illustrated in Montgomery, *Printed Textiles*, 1970, p.284. Copper roller 1459m.

Baker Record Sample A586

220 BONNY CHARLEY, copper roller-printed cotton, 1960
Drawn by Ernest Skinner, manufactured for the Williamsburg Restoration Inc. through F. Schumacher & Co.
36 × 34 (91 × 86) REPEAT: 29½ (75)

Reproduction of a late 1780s English printed handkerchief made into a repeating pattern. Red on white (see cat. 219).

Ernest Skinner worked in Bakers' studio from leaving school until his retirement in 1977. Copper roller 3292.

Baker Record Sample A587

221 SOLOMAN'S SEAL, copper roller-printed cotton, 1961
Drawn by Ernest Skinner, manufactured for the Williamsburg Restoration Inc. through F. Schumacher & Co.
33½ × 36½ (85 × 93) REPEAT: 36½ (93)

Trails of flowering plants in blue on white. Reproduction of a late 18th-century printed fabric from a quilt at Colonial Williamsburg. An original paper impression of this design is in the Bromley Hall pattern book p.24 in the V&A (E.458 (102, 103)-1955). Copper roller 1961m.

Baker Record Sample A630/3

222 Small samples of copper roller-printed silk dress fabrics 1952 to 1962
Various sizes and colourways

a. CHINESE SCHOOL HOUSE, first printed as a furnishing fabric in 1911. Copper roller 1298, an eight-colour print.
b. PERSIAN PANEL, first printed as a furnishing fabric in 1920. Copper roller 1736, an eight-colour print.
c. Small scattered rosebuds identical to those in the background of "Star of the Road" (cat. 218). Both fabrics were first printed in 1952. Copper roller 3143, a six-colour print.
d. Small floral motifs on a spotted ground with intertwining boughs bearing blossom and berries. First printed 1956. Copper roller, an eight-colour print.

Baker Record Samples C675, C40, no number and C712

223 NARCISSUS, copper roller-printed towelling, c.1962
A fragment

Same design as cat. 203. White, blue, yellow-green, dark green, grey and pink on pale yellow.

Baker Record Sample A598

*The following fabrics, cat. nos 224–247,** were all available in June 1983. The fabric width only is given and the date refers to the time when a design, or new version of an older design, first appeared on sale. They were all designed in Bakers' Studio, except for cat. nos 224 and 232.*

224 FERNS, screen-printed linen and cotton, since 1935
Designed by Joseph M. Doran
W. 55 (140) REPEAT: 25 (63)**

Twelve different varieties of fern said to be taken from botanical prints of ferns growing within a twelve mile radius of London's Mansion House, published in 1743.

This design has always remained popular. Originally block-printed (D81). Necessary alterations in size for screen-printing were carried out by photographic methods, it has never been redrawn.

Doran was a long established freelance designer of textiles and wallpapers. He covered a wide range of subject matter but by the late 1930s was best known and valued for his floral designs. His work is illustrated in Lewis *British Designers*. Another of his designs for Bakers was exhibited at Burlington House, 1935. Screen SC3474.

Baker pattern R1087

224

225 PROVENCAL, copper roller-printed cotton, since 1968
Adaptation drawn by Ernest Skinner
W. $49\frac{1}{4}$ (125) REPEAT: 8 (20)

Meandering stems and floral sprigs, a dainty small scale pattern taken from an 18th-century French dress print formerly in Bakers' possession.

Baker pattern A0683 (illus. p.133)

226 EMPEROR'S ROBE, screen-printed linen twill, since 1973
Designed by Ernest Skinner
W. 55 (140) REPEAT: $36\frac{1}{4}$ (92)

Repeating pattern of motifs taken from Chinese imperial dragon robes. The idea for this design came from "Pekin" (see cat. 161) but it is on a larger and grander scale. The designer studied fragments of Chinese textiles in Bakers' collection and consulted Mr Edmund Capon, then assistant keeper in the Far Eastern Department at the V&A. Screen SC2172.

Baker pattern R1053 (illus. p.132)

227 BOSONOVA, screen-printed linen twill, since 1973
Adaptation drawn by Gillian Spencer
W. 55 (140) REPEAT: $28\frac{1}{4}$ (72)

Geometric pattern of zig-zag stripes based on cat. 18. The design has been turned from the horizontal to the vertical. Screen SC2673.

Baker pattern R1068

228 THAMES BRIDGES, screen-printed cotton, since 1974
Designed by Philip Stockford
W. $49\frac{1}{4}$ (125) REPEAT: $38\frac{1}{2}$ (98)

Wallingford Bridge, Lechlade and other rural scenes interspersed with trails of convolvulus and honeysuckle. Composed from a series of 19th-century engravings (in Bakers' possession) of bridges on the upper reaches of the Thames.

Although the first screens were made in 1969 production of this design did not get underway until 1974 because of the difficulties in reproducing its fine lines and textures by screen.

Mr Stockford joined Bakers as a stylist in 1966 and became design director two years later after the death of Ronald Baker. He remained with the firm until 1979. His career before this had been varied. He had been an interior designer, stylist at Edward Turnbull & Sons Ltd., and set director for such films as "The Queen of Spades" and "Under Capricorn". Screen SC1969.

Baker pattern A0815

229 FEATHERS, screen-printed glazed cotton, since 1976
Adaptation drawn by Ann Lynch
W. 53 (135) REPEAT: 14 (36)

Light, airy columns of curling ostrich and other feathers, some speckled.

Originally a copper roller-print (2026) on cotton first produced in 1925. Screen SC175.

Baker pattern B0479 (illus. p.136)

230 BIRD AND THISTLE, screen-printed cotton, since 1976
Designed by Ann Lynch, manufactured for Brunschwig and Fils Inc., New York
W. 55 (140) REPEAT: 32 (82)

Meandering vertical stems sprouting a variety of leaves, including thistles and ferns, with perching song thrushes. Blue on white.

Reproduction of a 1780–85 plate-printed textile in the Winterthur collection, illustrated in Montgomery, *Printed Textiles*, p.51 and 250. Screen SC6575.

Baker pattern A0888

231 CHAO, swatch of screen-printed linen and cotton, since 1976
Designed by Ann Lynch
11 × 8 (28 × 20.5) REPEAT: 9 (23)

Small diaper pattern taken from the rim of a Chinese vase in the V&A.

Made to co-ordinate with "Chinese Waterlily" (no longer in production) which was inspired by the same vase and used the diaper pattern as a background.

Co-ordinating fabrics became popular in the early to mid 1970s.

Also produced as woven fabric, wallpaper and carpeting. Screen SC276.

Baker pattern R1123

Sample of Wilton Carpet
Mercia Weavers, Runcorn
10¼ × 7 (26 × 17.5)

Same design as above in shades of brown.

Lent by Mercia Weavers

232 ZARAND, sample swatch of screen-printed cotton, 1977
Adapted in an American studio
11 × 8 (28 × 20.5) REPEAT: 35½ (90)

Abstract design based on a 19th-century Turkoman chiné silk in Bakers' collection (L033). Screen SC876.

Baker pattern A0906

233 BAMBOO AND BLOSSOM, screen-printed cotton, since 1977
Designed by Ann Lynch
W. 55 (140) REPEAT: 32 (81)

Delicate design of flowering bamboo stems with butterflies and small birds.

Based on an 1820s block-printed cotton belonging to Bakers (H388).

Also produced as a wallpaper. Screen SC4777.

Baker pattern A0905 (illus. p.137)

234 TOUCANS, screen-printed glazed cotton, since 1977
Re-drawn by Liz Wright
W. 55 (140) REPEAT: 36 (91.5)

Exotic flowering trees with toucans, based on a chinese wallpaper now in Bakers' collection, see cat. 20.

The original design, by Turner, was block-printed (C685), using 105 blocks for each repeat, from 1922. It is illustrated in the *Studio Year Book*, 1925 and 1926. Screen SC6376.

Baker pattern B0499

235 CHERRY STRIPE, screen-printed glazed cotton, since 1978
Drawn by Barbara Edelman
W. 55 (140) REPEAT: 18 (45)

Redrawn from cat. 31. The new 1970s colouring of this design gives it quite a different impact from the original although the drawing is almost identical.

The same design was also printed in the 1940s and is illustrated in the *Ambassador* no.7 1952. Screen SC2777.

Baker pattern B0506

236 KIANGSU, screen-printed cotton, since 1979
Drawn by Claire Wooldridge and Philip Stockford
W. 55 (140) REPEAT: 32 (81)

Chinese floral design. The main motifs are taken from part of a Chinese painted silk hanging illustrated in Baker, *Calico Painting and Printing*, 1921, pl. 14.

The repeat of the original was almost twice the size of this version.

This is one of today's most popular designs. Screen SC4579.

Baker pattern A0948

237 HANKOW, screen-printed linen and cotton, since 1979
Re-drawn by Claire Wooldridge
W. 55 (140) REPEAT: 32½ (83)

Chinese vases and plants against a small geometric patterned background.

First block-printed (C503) from Turner's original design in 1914. It has been reprinted several times since. Screen SC3978.

Baker pattern R1167 (illus. p.140)

237a HAN, screen-printed linen and cotton, since 1979
Drawn by Claire Wooldridge
W. 55 (140) REPEAT: 8¼ (21)

Two-colour small repeating design taken from the background of above and produced specially to co-ordinate with it. Screen SC4078.

Baker pattern R1169 (illus. p.140)

238 PALAMPORE, screen-printed cotton, since 1980
Designed by Ann Lynch
W. 49¼ (125) REPEAT: 73 (185)

"Indian" floral design based on an Indian chintz given to the V&A by Bakers (IM.53-1919) and illustrated in Irwin, *Origins of Chintz*, 1970, p.74a.

Some of this fabric has been used for wallcoverings in the redecoration of Schloss Augustusberg Brühl, near Cologne.

Baker pattern A0945

239 MERMAID ROSE, screen-printed glazed cotton, since 1981
Drawn by Claire Wooldridge
W. 55 (140) REPEAT: 17½ (45)

Floral design of loose overblown roses, possibly French in origin.

First printed by Bakers in 1898 (block B582) when it was known as "Wild Rose'. Screen SC4879.

Baker pattern B0567

240 ROCKBIRD, screen-printed linen and cotton, since 1981
W. 55 (140) REPEAT: 35½ (90)

A Chinese inspired design of flowering magnolia tree, exotic flowers, rocks, pheasants and jungle birds.

Designed by William Turner and block-printed (C395) in seventeen colours in 1912. It has been reprinted many times since.

The same design was printed on a wallpaper, titled "The Golden Pheasant", by Jeffrey & Co. and is illustrated in the *Studio Year Book*, 1915. Screen SC4181.

Baker pattern R1035 (illus. p.141)

241 BAMBOO FOREST, screen-printed cotton, since 1981
Designed by Claire Wooldridge
W. 55 (140) REPEAT: 35½ (90)

Continuous design of bamboo stems adapted from a painted Indian cotton. Screen SC5779.

Baker pattern A0946

241a BAMBOO THICKET, screen-printed cotton, since 1981
Designed by Suzanne Akerman
W. 55 (140) REPEAT: 12½ (32)

Close-packed bamboo stems. Specially designed to co-ordinate with "Bamboo Forest". Screen SC4580.

Baker pattern A0947

242 GENOVESE, screen-printed glazed cotton, since 1982
Designed by Margaret Farmer
W. 55 (140) REPEAT: 32¼ (82)

Traditional English floral print with trailing cottage garden flowers and ribbon stripes.

Revival of block print B636 first printed about 1900. Screen SC4582.

Baker pattern B0597

242a RIGALIA, screen-printed glazed cotton, since 1982
Designed by Margaret Farmer
W. 55 (140) REPEAT: 16 (41)

All over pattern of interlooped ribbons. Designed to co-ordinate with "Genovese".

The design concept is derived from an 1840s printed cotton in Bakers' collection and there is also a similar pattern in Swaisland Book 18 about 1841–43.

Eleven colours are coded on the selvage. Screen SC4882.

Baker pattern B0589

243 SAKARI, screen-printed cotton, since 1982
Designed by Wendy Leighton
W. 55 (140) REPEAT: 32½ (83)

An imbricated pattern with uneven edges and varied filling patterns, with peacocks.

The motifs are taken from a 17th- or 18th-century painted Indian hanging illustrated in Baker, *Calico Painting and Printing*, 1921, pl. 3.

Baker pattern A0961 (illus. p.144)

242

242a

244 CASERTA, screen-printed cotton, 1983
Drawn by Wendy Leighton
W. 55 (140) REPEAT: $7\frac{1}{2}$ (19)

Small trellis design taken from a late 18th-century glazed cotton (Bakers' collection HY25 – not shown).

This pattern is also produced as a woven fabric for Bakers. Screen SC5983.

Baker pattern A0990

245 ORIENTAL GARDEN, screen-printed glazed cotton, 1983
Designed by Suzanne Akerman
W. 55 (140) REPEAT: $24\frac{3}{4}$ (63)

Doves perched on exotic flowering branches bearing bunches of grapes.

Based on a Chinese silk textile at Mulhouse. Screen SC6482.

Baker pattern B0606

246 CHINESE ASTRONAUTS, screen-printed cotton, 1983
Designed by Jane Griffiths
W. 55 (140) REPEAT: $25\frac{1}{4}$ (64)

Design taken from an 18th-century French block-printed cotton. Baker collection U250 (see cat. 48). Screen SC6082.

Baker pattern A0989

247 HYDRANGEA BIRD, screen-printed linen, 1983
Re-drawn by Jane Griffiths
W. $49\frac{1}{4}$ (125) REPEAT: 40 (102)

Magnificent pheasants in an exotic flowering tree.

First block-printed (C579) in 1916 from Turner's original design based on late 18th-century Chinese wallpaper.

A successful design which has remained in demand throughout this century.

Baker pattern R1026

248 NYMPHEUS, design for a printed textile, gouache on paper, about 1915
Designed by William Turner
$53\frac{1}{2} \times 32$ (136 × 82)

Water lilies with egret and kingfishers, based on cat. 19. Pale green and soft jade coloured leaves, light green flowers, grey green birds, touches of pink, and darker green background.

Design 1215 Baker Collection

248a NYMPHEUS, block-printed glazed cotton, 1915
Designed by William Turner
$53\frac{1}{2} \times 55$ (136 × 140) REPEAT: $41\frac{1}{4}$ (105)

Design as above but subtly coloured in palest greens, beiges and white. Parts of the design have a harder glaze. Block C575.

Baker Record Sample F642/5

248b NYMPHEUS, block-printed cotton, 1948–49
$17\frac{1}{2} \times 51\frac{1}{2}$ (44 × 131)

Same design as above in greys, yellow and white with a red background.

This colourway is probably a trial sample or a special order. Block as cat. 248a.

Baker Record Sample B93/2

248c NYMPHEUS, design for a printed textile, watercolour on paper, 1983
Drawn by Jo-Anne Wright
$49 \times 39\frac{1}{2}$ (124 × 100)

New version of cat. 248. Shades of green and slate blue with pinks, browns, blue black and small areas of bright blue and pale yellow. The background is a pale grey brown wash.

This light and airy watercolour contrasts sharply with Turner's heavy, gloomy gouache.

Baker Collection

248d NYMPHEUS, screen-printed linen, from Bakers' current range
W. $49\frac{1}{4}$ (125) REPEAT: 42 (107)

Screen SC9584.

Baker pattern R1131 (illus. on cover)

Nympheus is the Latin botanical name for a waterlily and an eastern waterlily is a lotus.

The following items are displayed in the technical section of the exhibition.

249 LOOM ENDS
Block-printed cottons, English, 1820–36
T.47 4 × 24 (10.1 × 61)
T.48 3 × 24 (7.6 × 61)

T.47 is stamped "Thos. Hoyle & Sons Manchester British Cambric". By 1797 the firm was established at Mayfield, Buxton Street, London Road. In 1804 they became Thomas Hoyle and Son, and from 1832–36 they were listed ". . . & Son*s*". The firm grew in importance throughout the 19th century with world-wide export markets including Constantinople. They were particularly renowned for their lilacs (information from J. Beckett, quoting J.T. Slugg, *Reminiscences of Manchester*, 1881). T.48 in blue and yellow check bears an illegible British Customs mark. The excise requirements of the first half of the 19th century ensured that much useful information is stamped on the ends of many printed cottons, providing certain attributions and dates.

V&A T.47 and T.48-1964 Given by G.P. & J. Baker Ltd.

250 PATTERN SAMPLE, block-printed cotton
Indian; possibly from Sangener, Jaipur, Rajastan; mid 19th century
45 × 32½ (114.3 × 82.5)

Small patterns in red and black are scattered at random. They include borders as well as centre fillings, floral motifs, birds, an elephant, sacred texts, "Vishnu's footprints" and other auspicious symbols suitable for use on Hindu prayer shawls (a local speciality) as well as motifs for general use on garments and furnishings. Among the inscriptions is one in Hindi "Babu Lal Chhap" [block printer] but he could be a merchant rather than the actual printer.

Baker No. E048

251 TROPICAL LEAF, block-printed linen, about 1929
53½ × 60 (136 × 152) REPEAT: 46½ (118)

Large leafed tree entwined with oleander, and other exotic jungle foliage in shades of pink, brown and grey-green, with blue parrots.

An oriental inspired design probably made 1910–20.

Baker Record Sample R119/3

251a Wood blocks used for printing "Tropical Leaf"
Various sizes

Purchased from Newman Smith & Newman of Dartford, Kent, when they went out of business in 1927.

Baker blocks DPW391. Baker Collection

252 PARADISE BIRD, copper roller-printed linen, 1961
Drawn by Ann Lynch, 1960
52 × 30½ (133 × 78) REPEAT: 23 (58)

Bird of paradise perching in an exotic flowering tree. Greens, browns, white, turquoise-green and coral pinks on pale beige.

One of William Turner's designs inspired by Chinese wallpapers, first block-printed (C624) on linen (P846) in 1918. Redrawn again in Bakers' studio in 1978 by Christine Stapleton for screen-printing.

Baker Record Sample R914/1 (illus. p.133)

252a Copper-roller used for printing above.
W. 31 (79)

One of the nine rollers for this design, one roller being required for each separate colour to be printed.

Engraved by Bakers at Crayford.

Bakers copper roller 3326

252b Wooden box containing engraving tools
Made by Allan Mingham
9¾ × 10¼ × 8¼ (25 × 26 × 21)

It was an established tradition for engravers to make their own tools. Mr Mingham worked for Bakers at Crayford and was their Foreman Engraver from 1957 until 1962.

Lent by Mr Allan Mingham

The Baker Studio

THE BAKER STUDIO AND ITS COLLECTION of archives has always been the very heart of the firm G.P. & J. Baker first of all at Swaislands of Crayford in Kent, and now in London.

In the past and still today the Studio bought from many well known designers who contributed greatly to broaden the Baker Image which was already beginning to veer towards the English floral. Among these designers were Lewis F. Day, Harry Napper, C.F.A. Voysey, Rex Silver and the brothers Turner, meanwhile in the Studio the beginnings of the team who were to create the "backbone" of the Baker Style which the general public today have come to recognise were establishing themselves. These were Thomas, Philip Reed and Ernest Skinner.

After the Second World War, Ronald Baker worked closely with both Philip Reed and Ernest Skinner in creating from the vast collection of archive designs which he then presented to his numerous clients across the world. Through the influence of Ronald Baker and these two designers the Studio developed and the toiles, oriental and chintz designs drawn almost exclusively in watercolour became the handwriting of G.P. & J. Baker.

The Studio being housed at Swaislands was a great asset as there was always a complete understanding between the printer and designer for the interpretation and method to which the design was destined. This philosophy was instilled into me firstly by Philip Reed and later by Ronald Baker who understood so well the joy of colouring a Baker product, which of course is the very essence of the Baker fabric today.

In 1964 the Studio moved to London after being purchased by the Parker Knoll Group, where it began to expand and with the death of Ronald Baker, Philip Stockford became Design Director until his retirement some five years ago.

The Baker Studio today has eight designers who carry on the art of drawing in watercolour and have the patience and pride to produce these documentary designs in the traditional style, with the added help of Audrey Duck who has taken on the mammoth task of conserving the archives.

Although the Studio is still following in the tradition of its forbears it is always looking to the future both in design and various methods of interpretation on the printed fabric whether it is a design drawn by the Studio or bought from an outside designer.

ANN LYNCH
Studio Manager and Colourist

Members of the Baker Studio today.

References

A&C Arts and Crafts Exhibitions. Held by the Arts and Crafts Exhibiting Society, London, from 1888 onwards.

Baker Calico Painting and Printing 1921 G.P. Baker, Calico Painting and Printing in the East Indies in the XVII–XVIII Centuries, London, 1921.

Baker Record Sample Fabric samples kept by the firm for reference.

Block Book Paper impressions recording what Bakers printed. Dates of recuts are noted with the codes for clients and occasionally a date. The earliest dates from 1893.

Boston Museum of Fine Arts, Boston, Mass. U.S.A.

British Textile Design 1980 Editors Donald King and Takahito Sano, British Textile Design in the Victoria and Albert Museum, 3 volumes, Tokyo, 1980.

Colonial Williamsburg Colonial Williamsburg Virginia, U.S.A.

Cotton Board 1955 Exhibition of English Chintz; two centuries of changing taste, Cotton Board Colour, Design and Style Centre, Manchester, 1955.

Dorland Hall 1933 Exhibition of British Industrial Art in relation to the home, Dorland Hall, London, 1933.

English Chintz 1960 Loan Exhibition of English Chintz, Victoria and Albert Museum, London, 1960.

Farnham 1982 Deryn O'Connor & Hero Granger-Taylor, Colour and the Calico Printer, an exhibition of printed and dyed textiles 1750–1850, West Surrey College of Art and Design, the Hart, Farnham, Surrey, September–October 1982, and Quarry Bank Mill, Styal, Cheshire, November–December 1982.

Fustian A material with a linen warp and a cotton weft. Many patterns were printed in England on fustian before the printing of all cotton cloth was legalised in 1774. The Act of 1774 also coincided with improvements in the spinning of a fine cotton warp.

Hunton English Decorative Textiles 1930 W. Gordon Hunton, English Decorative Textiles, Tapestry and Chintz, their design development from the earliest times to the 19th century, London, 1930.

Indian Heritage 1982 The Indian Heritage, Court Life under Mogul Rule, Victoria and Albert Museum, London, April–August 1982.

Irwin Golconda Cotton Paintings 1959 John Irwin, Golconda Cotton Paintings of the early 17th century, Lalit Kala no. 5, April 1959.

Irwin and Brett Origins of Chintz 1970 J. Irwin and K. Brett, Origins of Chintz, London, 1970.

Jacqué Mulhouse 1978 J.T. Jacqué, V. de Bruignac & T. Sano, Musée de L'Impression sur Etoffes, Tome 11, Imprimés français 11, Européens et Orientaux, Tokyo, 1978.

Lewis British Designers 1941 Frank Lewis, British Textile Designers: Their Work, Leigh-on-Sea, 1941.

Libertys 1975 Liberty's 1875–1975, Victoria and Albert Museum, London, July–October 1975.

Manchester Whitworth Art Gallery, Manchester.

Metropolitan Museum Metropolitan Museum of Art, New York, U.S.A.

Metropolitan Museum 1927 A retrospective exhibition of painted and printed fabrics, Metropolitan Museum of Art, New York, 1927.

Montgomery Printed Textiles 1970 Florence M. Montgomery, Printed Textiles, English and American Cottons and Linens 1700–1850, London, 1970.

Oman & Hamilton Wallpapers 1982 C.C. Oman & J. Hamilton. Wallpapers, a History and Illustrated Catalogue of the Collection in the V&A Museum, London, 1982.

Paris 1925 International Exhibition of Modern Decorative and Industrial Arts, Paris, 1925.

RIBA Royal Institute of British Architects.

RIBA Symonds 1976 Joanna Symonds, Catalogue of drawings by C.F.A. Voysey in the Drawings Collection of the Royal Institute of British Architects, 1976.

Studio Year Book Studio Year Book of Decorative Arts.

Stuttgart 1980 Art Nouveau, Textil Dekor um 1900, Württembergischen Landesmuseum, Stuttgart July–August 1980 (afterwards taken to Vienna, Lyon and Prato).

Tilliet Marie-François Tilliet, Tissus Anglais aux Musées Royaux d'Art et d'Histoire: de William Morris à l'Art Nouveau, Bulletin des Musées Royaux d'art et d'Histoire, Bruxelles, 1978.

Toronto Royal Ontario Museum, Toronto, Canada.

Tuchscherer 1972 J.-M. Tuchscherer, The Fabrics of Mulhouse and Alsace 1801–1850, Leigh-on-Sea, 1972.

Voysey 1978 C.F.A. Voysey: architect and designer 1857–1941, Brighton Art Gallery and Museum, July–September 1978 (afterwards at Wolverhampton).

V&A Victoria and Albert Museum, London.

V&E DA 1952 Exhibition of Victorian and Edwardian Decorative Arts, Victoria and Albert Museum, London, 1952.

Winterthur Henry Francis Dupont Winterthur Museum, Delaware, U.S.A.

Footnotes

G.P. & J. Baker – a prologue

1 Prospectus – Companies House.

2 Layard, the archaeologist, was originally employed to survey and map the frontier – but requested leave of absence to work at Nineveh. PRO.FO.802 index of correspondence. p.705. July 1848. He was sent back to England in May 1849.

3 PRO.FO.196.27. Misc letter book 1845–6.

4 PRO.FO.196.27. May 24th 1845.

5 PRO.FO.196.27 Sir Stratford Canning to Sir Edward Owen in Malta.

6 One of a collection of loose letters mostly dating from 1875–7 between George senior or Charles Edwards in Constantinople and G.P. in London.

7 PRO.FO.196.27 p.327. Letter to Major Rawlinson, March 25th 1846.

8 PRO.FO.802. April 1845, p.632 etc.

9 Letters, October 30th 1876 and November 3rd 1876 from Charles Edwards to G.P. Baker.

10 September 1st 1876. Charles Edwards to G.P. Baker.

11 Sir Alexander Telford Waugh. *Turkey, yesterday, today and tomorrow*, 1930 p.90, and other memoirs consulted include Fanny, Lady Blunt, *My Reminiscences* 1918 and those of Halidé Edib 1926.

12 *Levant Herald* Tuesday, June 14th 1870. We are very much indebted to Mrs V. Carnegy-Arbuthnott for searching the foreign language newspapers of the period in Istanbul for any references to the Bakers.

13 PRO.FO.78.3206. Correspondence on the Embassy Buildings in Therapia and Constantinople. Treasury letter May 19th 1849.

14 Letter Book 1886–7, p.652, November 9th 1887.

15 Letter Book 1886–7, p.838v, April 14th 1888.

16 *Levant Herald* Thursday January 2nd 1868.

17 Letter Book, p.903, June 1888. James frequently had trouble filling his father's orders. "Smith's patent lavatory" nearly defeated him. "There are over 2000 Smiths, $\frac{1}{4}$ Thomas and $\frac{1}{8}$ hold companies – it will save me a lot of time if you can give an address and an idea as to price . . . a soufflet dish what price am I to pay . . .?" In July he told his father that the soufflet dish would have to be specially made.

18 October 24th 1875 and March 28th 1876.

19 Army & Navy Stores
Bon Marché, Paris
Crosslands'
Debenham and Freebody
Hampton's
Harvey Nichols
Howell & James
Liberty
Printemps of Paris
Marshall, Lewis & Allenby
Marshall & Snelgrove
Welch Margetson

20 Benguiat – though they also traded with him.
Cardinal's (Cardinal and Harford)
Griffiths
"Hampton's man"
Levi Brothers
Maples
Shoolbred
Zieglers (this firm handled the Ardabil carpet now in the V&A)
Ziegler & Brown

21 d'Andria.
Sydney La Fontaine
Ali Molo
Members of the Baker family

22 Letter Book, p.613, September 17th 1887.

23 Letter Book, p.490, May 14th 1887.

24 Letter Book, p.469, April 23rd 1887.

25 Letter Book, p.469, April 23rd 1887.

26 Letter Book, p.725, December 31st 1887.

27 Letter Book, p.692, December 7th 1887.

28 Letter Book, p.337, January 11th 1887.

29 Letter Book, p.91, May 4th 1886.

30 Letter Book, p.308v, December 15th 1886.

31 Letter Book, p.460, April 16th 1887.

32 Letter Book, p.489, May 14th 1887.

33 Letter Book, p.412, March 9th 1887.

34 Letter Book, p.417, March 12th 1887.

35 Letter Book, p.590, September 7th 1887.

36 Letter Book, p.377v, January 19th 1887.

37 Letter Book, p.508, May 28th 1887.

38 Letter Book, p.268, November 6th 1886.

39 Letter Book, p.456, April 6th 1887.

40 Letter Book, p.293, November 27th 1886.

41 Letter Book, p.450, April 1887.

42 Letter Book, p.939, August 18th 1888.

43 Letter Book, p.270, November 6th 1886.

44 Letter Book, p.794, March 3rd 1888.

45 Letter Book, p.850, April 25th 1888.

46 Letter Book, p.863, April 26th 1888.

47 Letter Book, p.838v, April 14th 1888.

Pattern-Books and Precursors

1 P.R.O. Kew. B.T.44/17. Registrations of designs show changes more minutely than annual directories.

2 G.C. Haité, Design and Designers of the Victorian Reign, in the *Architectural Review*, vol. II, 1897, pp.81–9.

3 M. Clayton and A. Oakes, Early Calico Printers around London, in the *Burlington Magazine*, vol. XCVI, 1954, pp.135–9.

4 G.P. Baker once had an order-book said to contain dealings of the Wares with Amos Swaisland in 1789, a date too late for the Wares, but possible for an ancestor of Charles Swaisland, who in 1844–5 was registering designs in partnership with a younger Amos Swaisland.

5 S.D. Chapman, The last of the old London Textile Printers, in *Textile History*, vol. 14, No. 1, Spring 1983, pp.29–56 (p.37).

6 Kent R.O., Lease U 1567 T7.

7 S. Bagshaw, *Directory of Kent*, 1847, vol. I, pp.666–7.

8 Loans to V&A, nos 7, 8, 9 (cat. 51), 10, 11. Martin Baker has a booklet of

designs in a binding marked "Vint & Gilling". In 1793 Gilling, Hilliard & Rivers and Edward Vint were both printing at Crayford. Could the Rivers of that firm be part of the Howard, Rivers & Co. of Mitcham in 1808? (V&A loan 3, see cat. 41). Other names on books in the Swaisland archive include William Fenning & Sons; Moore, Johnstone & Mason of Wandsworth; and Henry Cooke, woollen printer (valencias).

9 Bagshaw, op. cit.

10 The cotton goods described in S.D. Chapman (op. cit., p.37) seem likely to be products of the 1870s–80s, on a par with export goods printed at Swaisland's for Bakers'.

11 *The Journal of Design*, vol. I, March 1849, p.6.

12 1851 Exhibition. Reports of the Juries, pp.380–1. Slightly less elaborate Swaisland shawls of the 1840s, which led up to his 1851 success, can be seen in the temporary exhibition in the V&A Dress Collection (Room 40) until Spring 1985.

13 Library Pressmark, Box III, 86DD(x).

14 The Public Record Office fortunately preserves the complete designs of the larger shawls.

15 G.C. Haité, op. cit.

The Baker Family

1 G.P. Baker, typewritten document, written in 1945. Ruby K. Gray, *The George Baker Family*, published in 1965 (Ruby Gray was the daughter of Arthur Baker). *The History of G. & A. Baker*, written in 1968.

2 Their children were Katherine, Ellen and James (born before 1820 when the family moved to Totteridge); Francis (1820); George (1822); Emma (1824); Mary (1827); John (1830); and Alfred (1833).

3 Researched by Miss Natalie Rothstein at the British Embassy in Istanbul. Albert was not registered but is noted in the family tree devised by May Morton (Arthur's daughter) and Robin Baker in 1957/8.

4 On Charles Edward's death in 1899, Middleton, his son, took charge of the company assisted by his younger brother Cecil, who described the development of trade in his influential book *The Persian Carpet*, published in 1953.

5 Cyril had been destined for a career with O.C.M. and, before enlisting in the army, had been in charge of the firm's Agency at Meshed, Persia.

6 These included Sikh, Fleur D'Amor, Khoosroo, Saphire, Basque Violet, Diosma, Aga Khan, Nizam, Fraternity, Magnum, Violet Bonnet, Sadee, Granny, Maid of Kent, Omer, Khalifah, Zingari, Zuleika, Iraki, Kismet, Kamet, Mardi, Zenobia and Nazir.

G.P. & J. Baker – the first twenty years

1 Letters from G.P. Baker written whilst travelling show large orders for embroideries in Broussa and Aleppo in particular, despite bad feeling amongst local traders. Of Broussa he wrote "Gold work is 30% better than Consple [Constantinople]. I have bought £130 and given orders". From Constantinople "I am prevailing upon our people to Employ a special hand to look after the whole work". Aleppo covers were very popular and one order consisted of "20 blue green, 20 pink, 20 lemon, 20 coffee, 20 cream, 20 other, 50 piece gold thread . . . 200 pieces altogether".

2 Letter dated December 11th 1877. Baker Collection.

3 Wardle refers to Morris in his letter to Baker saying that he could not do the same kind of work without his permission. It is likely that he referred to natural dyestuffs for which, by 1877, he and Morris had revived a number of techniques.

4 G.P. Baker's memoirs, a typewritten draft made for the family.

5 Although this lies north of the other factory which formed the Swaisland Works, it was downstream from it.

6 In an article in a local Crayford paper on the occasion of the Golden wedding of Mr and Mrs G.P. Baker in 1934, G.P. listed the first workmen as "Mr John Doyle, Mr John Foreman, Mr W. Thomas, Mr Dan Murphy, Mr W. Corke, Mr W. Foreman, Mr T. Webb and Mr C. Tagg whose forebears were printers at Hall Place in 1780. Of these the four latter only survive and Mr W. Drew is still in the employment of the firm".

7 Sale undertaken by Wheatley, Kirk, Price and Goultry on Wednesday–Friday, January 25th–27th 1893. A telegram from Doyle to G.P. Baker at Ivy Lane asking advice on lots has been kept with the catalogue.

8 Harold Clayton (1875–1950) was apprenticed to the Low Printing Co., Whittle-le-Wood, Chorley. He subsequently worked as a chemist and lecturer on printing and dyeing techniques at the Royal Technical College, Salford. So impressed was G.P. Baker with his credentials that he travelled to Manchester to interview Clayton, the meeting taking place in the Midland Hotel.

9 Percy Pulman resigned on December 31st 1910 before this term was finished.

10 March 28th 1893 (209883) unidentified modern floral design; November 8th 1893 (222011) "Tulip Tree"; November 22nd 1893 (222725) "Scutari"; February 23rd 1894 (227987) "Thrush", a Voysey design; (227988–227990) all Turkish influenced designs.

11 Charles C. Oman and Jean Hamilton *Wallpapers*, 1982.

12 V&A design E.59-1961 and designs in the Baker Collection. See also illustrations in *Der Moderne Stil* magazine.

13 See *Jahrbuch der Staatlichen Kunstsammlungen in Baden-Württenberg* 18–1981, p.207.

14 "Twyford" was used by Mortons as "Aira" gauze in 1904. "Grape and Vine" as "Phyllis" woven wool. "Scylla" and "Thorley" were also used by other manufacturers (see *Der Moderne Stil IV*).

15 Baker machine number 815. Illustrated in Liberty's catalogue *Furnishing Fabrics*, 1906.

16 *The Furnisher* magazine, October 1900, p.92. *The Queen* magazine, November 28th 1903, p.915.

G.P. & J. Baker – 1914 onwards

1 *The Studio Year Book of Decorative Art*, London 1927, p.167, and 1928, p.181.

2 Sir Frank Warner and A.F. Kendrick *Reports on the Industrial Arts as Indicated at the International Exhibition of Modern Decorative and Industrial Arts, Paris, 1925*. Department of Overseas trade 1927, p.96.

3 R.R.R. "Lesser Country Houses of Today – Norman House, Stansted, Essex" *Country Life* magazine, March 1927, p.372.

4 "Cloth Printing at the Swaislands Works" in the *Cabinet Maker and Complete House Furnisher;* May 13th 1933, p.233.

5 Fuller descriptions of these printing methods can be found in Edmund Knecht and James Best Fothergill *The Principles and Practice of Textile Printing*, C. Griffin & Co. Ltd., London, 1912 and Joyce Storey *A Thames and Hudson Manual of Textile Printing*, Thames and Hudson Ltd., London, 1974.

6 D.W.H. Burtonshaw "Textile Printing" in *Textile Magazine* vol. 12, no. 2, p.44 summer 1983, the Shirley Institute, Manchester, England.

7 This story was related by George Davies, Bakers' present European Sales Director. Mr Bloch's son-in-law, Albert Modiano, is one of the European agents.

8 *The Studio Year Book* 1937, p.139.

9 Grace Lovat Fraser, "Interior Decoration and Furnishing in 1939" in *The Studio Year Book*, 1940, p.43.

10 "A point of view" in the *Ambassador* magazine, London, no. 7, July 1952, p.74.

11 "Cloth-Printing at the Swaislands Works" in the *Cabinet Maker and Complete House Furnisher*, May 13th 1933, p.231.

12 *The Kentish Times*, Friday, August 30th 1963.

13 Michael Cutcliffe is responsible for markets in English speaking countries. Europe was taken care of by Leslie Packer, previously Parkertex export manager. George Davies joined the firm as European sales manager in 1966 and became a director in 1976. Barry Thick, home sales manager, was made marketing director at the same time.

Acknowledgements

We are grateful to the Trustees of the British Museum for the loan of cat. 19, to Mr John Harris, Curator of the Drawings Collection of the British Architecture Library of the RIBA for the loan of cat. 95, to the Musées Royaux d'Art et d'Histoire, Brussels, for the loan of cat. nos 97, 99, 101, 103, 112, to Mr Allan Mingham for the loan of engraving tools, cat. 252B, and to Mr Martin Baker for information and for the loan of family papers and cat. nos. 1–7, 78, 79.

We should also like to thank the Librarian of the Royal Horticultural Society, Mr C. Baker, Assistant Curator, Dartford Museum, Mr Jeremy Barbour-Hill of the Science Museum, Mrs V. Carnegy-Arbuthnott for her work on the Bakers in Turkey, Mr Arthur Edwards for information about his father, A. Cecil Edwards, Miss Barbara Tomlinson of the National Maritime Museum for identifying the scene in cat. 10, Mr Mark Turner, Curator of the Silver Studio of Middlesex Polytechnic, Ms Christine Waterman, Assistant Curator, Hall Place, Bexley, and our colleagues Mr Robert Skelton and Miss Veronica Murphy of the Indian Department for their help on the Indian textiles cat. nos. 14, 15, 16, Miss Verity Wilson of the Far Eastern Department, Miss Levey and all members of the Department of Textiles and Dress for their encouragement and forbearance and, especially, Mrs Valerie Mendes and Miss Linda Woolley for co-ordinating our activities and the staff of Bakers Studio likewise. We should also like to thank our two photographers Paul Fox and Philip Barnard.